UNWANTED HARVEST?

EVENTUALLY, EVERY CHRISTIAN WILL ENCOUNTER SOMEONE WHO IS STRUGGLING WITH HOMOSEXUALITY. YOUR RESPONSE IS CRITICAL TO ENCOURAGING THEIR HEALING AND WALK WITH GOD.

UNWANTED HARVEST?

MONA RILEY and BRAD SARGENT

BROADMAN
& HOLMAN
PUBLISHERS

Nashville, Tennessee

Printed in the United States of America

Published by:
Broadman & Holman Publishers
Nashville, Tennessee

Design by:
Steven Boyd
4261-56
0-8054-6156-6

Dewey Decimal Classification: 261.835
Subject Heading: Church Work with Homosexuals
Library of Congress Card Catalog Number: 95-12240

The stories that appear in this book are based on the lives of real people. In some cases, the names and minor details have been changed to protect the identity of those individuals.

Unless noted otherwise, Scripture quotations are from the King James Version of the Bible.

Library of Congress Cataloging-in-Publication Data
Riley, Mona, 1951–
    Unwanted harvest? / Mona Riley, Brad Sargent
        p.   cm.
    ISBN 0-8054-6156-6 (hardbound)
        1. Homosexuality—Religious aspects—Christianity—
Controversial literature. 2. Homosexuality—Moral and ethical
aspects. 3. Church work with gays. I. Sargent, Brad, 1955– .
II. Title.
    BR115.H6S27   1995
    261.8'35766—dc20

    95-12240
    CIP

    99 98 97 96 95 5 4 3 2 1

Contents

Acknowledgments

ACKNOWLEDGMENTS NEVER SAY ENOUGH, NOR DO THEY THANK ALL those deserving. So we begin with an apology to those whose names and deeds are not recorded here.

Mona wishes to thank the following:

John Smid, Mike Haley, Dawn Killion, Tim Rymel, and John and Ann Paulk from Love In Action, who graciously consented to be interviewed and also provided constructive help in shaping *Unwanted Harvest?* Many other men and women who gave of their time and shared sensitive things about their lives, choosing to be written about with a pseudonym. Henry Dalehite, who gave me a computer, and Bob Case, who started me on the machinery and kept the wheels turning. Iva Conrad, Bob Davies, and Jean Hartley, who have been good teachers.

My church family at Church of the Open Door in San Rafael, California.

And my family—Michael, Jared, Jonathan, Becky, and Deborah. And of course, Daddy, Mom, Gram, Raymond, Gussie, and my sisters and brother.

Brad wishes to thank the following:

Dr. Lalia Phipps Boone, who taught me how to edit; Elaine Wright Colvin and Christine Tangvald, long-time nurturers of me as a writer; my parents, Victor and Rowena Sargent, who always believed in me and what I was doing; and my sister Romae, who somehow always knew I was a writer; Harold Ivan Smith, whom God used as a catalyst to spark my action in the AIDS ministry. Jonathan Hunter and Beth Webb, who serve as sounding boards for me personally and in my HIV-related work.

My coworkers at Exodus—Bob Davies, Kevin Oshiro, and Claire Ezekiel—who kept encouraging me to persevere. Dave Johnson, who put up with my rantings and ravings, and the late-night computer sounds.

My two church families—BayMarin Community Church in San Rafael, California, especially the Tuesday Night Family Group; and South Hill Bible Church in Spokane, Washington.

Together, we would like to thank:

Vicki Crumpton, our editor at Broadman & Holman, for her consistent advocacy for *Unwanted Harvest?*

The persevering men and women who served as our prayer and encouragement team. Truly, without their support, *Unwanted Harvest?* could not have become a reality. Our deep thanks go to Peg Aten; Patricia Baldwin; Laurette Beale; Barbara Berreman; Pam Booker; Rick and Kathy Bradley; Lanny Broadwell; Bob and Mary Busha; Randy, Beth, Ryan, and Tyler Carey; JoAnn Crews; Barbara Decker; Debbie Duberow; Diane Ellison; Nanette Fenn; Mark Gebhardt; Bob, Donna, Christopher, Mark, and Shawn Gilliland; Glee Helms; Bob, Patti, Karisse, and Aletha Hendrick; Lynn Hensel; Rick Hocker; Ava Hoffman; Jonathan Hunter; Kristy Keith; Laura Lee Justus; Patti Justus; Ilona League; Janet LeBlond; Marion Meek; Karl and Michele Methum; Donna Miller; Steve O'Steen; Pam Owen; Helen Mae Reed; Steve and Mimi Reed; Maggie Ricciardi; Bob and Pam Rising; Phil and Jeanne Rosenbaum; Deb Roy; Judy Ruminski; Peggy Secundo; Marion Smith; Jeff Sutter; Ray and Mary Veal; Beth Webb; Pat and Maryanne Wendt; and Melanie White.

Introduction:
An Opportunity for Ministry

HOMOSEXUALITY IS ONE OF THE HOTTEST SOCIAL ISSUES OF THE nineties, and it may well serve as the barometer of how Christians in local churches reach their surrounding community for Christ. If we are obedient in reaching out, sooner or later someone from a homosexual or lesbian background will enter our fellowship. Are we ready, or will the shocked response of some church members convey the impression that these individuals are unwanted and unwelcomed? How can Christians learn to reach out with truth, love, and hope to men and women entangled in a gay lifestyle?

This decade has been labeled the Gay Nineties both by the gay community and various media. The theologically conservative wing of the church has reacted with a wave of newsletters, books, videotapes, lectures, and political action groups. But is the church being salt and light in our culture? Do we mean it when we sing about people coming to God "just as I am"? Are we helping those who want out of their bondage?

So many complex issues and questions! To begin addressing these problems, we wrote *Unwanted Harvest?* This book arises from our own experiences, so let us introduce ourselves and how this book came into being.

I [Mona] grew up surrounded by gay people. My father owned The Black Cat Cafe—a notoriously flambouyant San Francisco gay bar—from 1949 until 1963, when the state of California shut it down. Though not a homosexual himself, my father accepted gays, lesbians, and other people just as they were. He did this although he believed homosexuality was wrong and upheld a different standard for his children. Believing no one should single out a specific group for discrimination, my father became a civil rights and gay rights advocate long before the militant gay rights movement began.

So, from childhood, I possessed an unfearful, unprejudiced knowledge of gay people and gained the background for later becoming a spiritual rights and "ex-gay" rights advocate as a Christian. In God's providence, I married Mike Riley, who became senior pastor at Church of the Open Door in San Rafael, California. This church, birthed out of the hippie era, sponsored Love In Action, one of the world's first ministries to people leaving a gay lifestyle.

Until Love In Action moved to Memphis, Tennessee, in 1994, I participated consistently in this unique ministry. I observed a steady stream of ex-gays and ex-lesbians go through Love In Action's support groups and live-in discipleship programs. I have prayed for the men, counseled with the women, and seen some flounder and others prosper. And, since several congregation members have loved ones actively engaged in a gay lifestyle, I also know the hurts. I have been around formerly homosexual men and women, and their loved ones, nearly all of my adult Christian life.

I became burdened for *Unwanted Harvest?* because I saw first-hand how much love and acceptance meant in those who came to Love In Action. I knew Christians must respond to this need! That meant I had to respond. At a writer's conference, an editor recommended I write this book. "Do you know Brad Sargent?" she asked. I had to laugh. Brad had been in our church, and we had already worked together on another project. "You might consider collaborating with him," she suggested. And I did.

I [Brad] became interested in a Christian response to HIV/AIDS before knowing a single person who was infected with, or had full-blown AIDS. Then within nine months of attending my first HIV ministry training seminar in 1989, the Christian AIDS Service Alliance invited me to join their board of directors. This referral and resource network of theologically conservative churches and HIV/AIDS ministries officially began in 1990, though its roots go back to the mid-1980s. It offered the biblical perspective I was looking for—compassion for people affected by HIV, but without compromise regarding possibly sinful activities that resulted in their contracting the HIV disease.

I have served since 1990 as secretary-treasurer for CASA, and I edit its quarterly newsletter. Occasionally I teach at churches and conferences on AIDS. My bibliographies and articles on HIV/AIDS have seen wide circulation within HIV ministry circles. I also helped start a mail-order book service for Christian materials on AIDS.

In addition, I work as the resource/publication specialist for Exodus International, a referral network of "ex-gay" ministries. I also have had significant input editing three manuscripts for men and women overcoming homosexuality. Besides expertise on AIDS, I am growing in my knowledge of men's gender identity and sexuality disorders and the biblical route to transformation. Much of my interest in gender and sexuality topics stems from my own wrestling with the question of what it means to be a Christlike man, and with the issue of homosexual feelings I never "acted out."

Since becoming a Christian in 1974, I can testify that God has revolutionized my thought-life. This has taken place gradually as I have submitted myself to Him.

So the reader will know who is "speaking," Mona wrote chapters 1 through 10 and chapters 13 through 16. I edited Mona's chapters and contributed some of the resource material she used. I also wrote chapters 11 and 12 dealing specifically with AIDS.

Our desire in writing this book is to educate fellow Christians about the need for compassionate ministry to those trying to overcome homosexuality. We have seen that it can be done, for we have witnessed God changing the lives of men and women. This book is also a testimony that the Lord's power can reach and transform any and every life. He is the Vinedresser who picks and prunes even those vines that others may overlook. With God, there is no unwanted harvest.

PART ONE

Compassion without Compromise

CHAPTER ONE

The Harvest Begins with Me: Dealing with Personal Prejudgments

I STRAIGHTENED THE ROW OF TINY BOTTLES CAREFULLY, SNAPPED the door shut, and moved to the next display case. The early morning quiet of the cosmetics department was always good for housekeeping. In five years I had learned that few women ventured into the world of beauty-for-sale until they looked their best, and that was rarely in the morning.

"Excuse me, please," a man's voice spoke softly behind me.

I turned and smiled. "Yes. Can I help you?"

"Well. . . ." He hesitated, looked around, and smiled uneasily. "I need some makeup," he whispered.

Unthinking, I countered, "What kind of makeup?" Then almost laughing, "Is it for you?"

His hands resting on the counter fluttered, leaving large wet fingerprints on the glass beneath them.

"Oh," he began. "It's for . . . well, do you have anything that will cover my beard?" The question burst out in one rush of breath. His eyes begged for understanding. Small beads of sweat stood out on his brow and upper lip.

Though clean-shaven, the jowly face before me, *did* show a bluish tinge of beard. I hesitated, somewhat embarrassed.

His anxious gaze, meeting no understanding, dropped to his hands. A small sigh escaped. "I don't know what to do," he said quietly. "Most stuff I've figured out, but I can't seem to get rid of my beard. It ruins my looks."

As strange and repugnant as the request sounded, it wasn't the first time I had heard it.

Flashback to San Francisco

Memory washed over the present: My mother, cozy in her bathrobe, feet drawn up on the couch, was giving herself a pedicure. The huge picture windows of our San Francisco home danced with nighttime shadows.

The windows in the apartment downstairs were dark this evening. Of the four gay men who shared the flat, only Carl was home from work. A small, plump man with a ready laugh and uncomplicated eyes, he often came upstairs to watch television with us.

Now, seated in the chair near my mother, he complained, "I mean, my dear Candy, you can't know how hard it is to cover a beard. You must have some ideas. My face is raw with trying to scrape it away. But then I can't find a makeup to hide the blue without resorting to pancake, ugh!"

Laughing, she asked, "Why don't you go to a department store downtown? They'd be able to tell you how to correct for color problems."

"Ahhh," he shrieked. "Do you want me to die in my prime? You're such an innocent! Those women would *eat me alive* if I ever asked them for help with makeup! No, thank you. I'll keep getting my cosmetics from the drug store. At least there they don't care who or what you are."

My Age of Innocence

My earliest childhood memories included many such scenes. The bar my father, Sol Stoumen, owned was a well-known hangout for all sorts of people who did not fit society's norms. Artists and bohemians rubbed shoulders and shared drinking time with gays and lesbians in the colorful Barbary Coast backdrop of The Black Cat Cafe in San Francisco. Many were family friends who regularly visited our home. Some worked for my dad.

As children, we usually referred to them as our aunts and uncles. We related to gay people on a daily basis. I did not realize until my teen years that other people did not have the same experiences.

The atmosphere from the late 1940s to the 1960s was unfriendly to gay people, even in San Francisco. My father was constantly involved in court battles, trying to protect the civil rights of this very unpopular minority—and to keep his bar open. I did not understand what it was all about until decades later—but I did know that often neighbors shunned our family and that my father was the object of their distaste. As a child, I had assumed their displeasure was because my father was Jewish.

I later learned many people assumed my father was gay himself. He was not, nor did he believe a homosexual lifestyle was acceptable before his God. Being of Russian Jewish parentage, he was raised to hold a biblical standard on this issue.

My Two Fathers' Standards

Anger suffused Sol's face the day my brother played dress-up with us girls. "Go and take that dress off," he ordered. "A man never dresses as a woman. It's wrong!" Though my brother was young, he obeyed immediately.

Once I asked, "Daddy, if it's wrong to be a homosexual, why are you helping them?"

"Baby, it is wrong, but it's a personal choice a man makes. These guys are welcome to work for me and drink here with their friends, no matter who or what they are. Look at Max. He's an alcoholic. I think that's wrong, too. But I don't refuse him service and the government doesn't care how many alcoholics meet here. No, we single out this one group to punish because they're so different. That's not right."

Years later, as a Christian I was still proud of my father's accomplishments. They took on a new significance to me in the early 1970s when our church sponsored a pilot project helping gay men walk away from their lifestyle. Now I felt I had a real stake in what Sol Stoumen had stood for.

Men and women battling to overcome their homosexuality longed for acceptance and allies in their fight. By God's grace they found both in Love In Action and at Church of the Open Door in San Rafael, California.

Through the involvement of the Love In Action ministry in our church, I realized that my Heavenly Father was a spiritual rights advocate for the "ex-gay" men and women in His family. His will included their full participation in the church family.

Of course, God upholds a different, righteous standard for His children. He expects them to fully abandon their former gay and lesbian lifestyles to follow Christ. That is the only way they will ever see His desires and design for their lives fulfilled.

Hiding What We Do Not Want to See

As strongly as I believed in this new ministry and what my father taught us, it never occured to me that I still had prejudices in this area. After nearly three decades of being around gays and lesbians, including several more years around Christian men and women leaving homosexuality, how could I still have an unloving attitude?

But now, faced with a test in the form of this gay man wanting makeup, I saw how much more work was needed in my life. Hired to sell cosmetics, I did not have the prerogative to turn away prospective customers based on my view of their lifestyles. How could I do an effective job, either as a Christian or a makeup consultant, with a smile frozen on my face and no compassion in my heart?

Lord, I prayed, *help me with this one. If ever a man needed Your love, this fellow does. I don't feel like I have it for him.*

With what I hoped was a good mixture of kindness and dignity, I began. "You need to start with a color-corrective moisturizer . . ."

Oh, Lord. What am I doing, putting makeup on this man?

"Blend it down carefully at the neckline and around the edges of your beard . . ."

Blend it down around the edges of your beard? This can't be right!

"Now apply a light layer of foundation. This is a good color for you."

This man is pathetic, Lord. Here I am—helping him pick colors!

"Once you've blended down the foundation, finish with a light powder."

Okay. So I've helped this guy cover his beard. He's smiling. He thinks I like helping him. I've totally fooled him into believing I'm compassionate and understanding.

"The blush goes on next. Oh, fine. You've got it from here."

Suddenly it was as if I had heard another voice.

Mona?

Yes, Lord?

Why aren't you compassionate
and understanding?

What?

What makes you think this man
is a greater sinner than all the women
you wait on all day?

Lord, this guy is gay! Your Word says that's an abomination!

So is your pride, but I still love you.
You know something about his sin, that's all.
You've judged it to be worse.
Everyone who comes to this counter is a sinner.
You manage to help them without the kind
of disgust you're feeling for this man.
I love this man. I created him in My image, too.

It was true. I had used the same combination of products many times to help women cover scars and birthmarks. Not a week before, a young girl stood before me, asking for the same cosmetics.

"But your birthmark is hardly noticeable," I had tried to encourage.

"I feel so ugly, though," she insisted. "I just want to hide it until I'm old enough to have it removed."

I felt such empathy for her! She was clearly hurting. But so was this man. He viewed his masculinity as a bad birthmark instead of a bold birthright. Yes, he was wrong, but so was I. My attitude, my lack of genuine love, neutralized any Christian witness I might have had with him.

Now, examining his face in the small oval mirror, he smiled. "Oh, yes. Thank you so much! I've been so afraid to come and ask for help."

In retailing terms it was a good sale.

But what about in ministry terms? What could I have done differently? How could I have changed to be more responsive to his hurt and less reactive to his faults?

The cosmetics world exists to cover and hide. People do not come there for truth. No one expects a makeup artist to judge the right or wrong of wearing cosmetics. In fact, our every expectation is to receive help in covering our flaws, of hiding what we don't want seen.

But what happens when a man or woman comes into our church, horribly disfigured by sin? Need we examine in detail all the aspects of their particular sin? Or is it enough that they desire to change and have come for help? Do we—should we—turn them away? Or is that never our prerogative if we are reaching the world with the good news of salvation in Jesus Christ?

Perspectives and Presumptions

Because of my background in cosmetics, Christian women who have not used makeup before and now want to try will occasionally ask me to teach them. Often, these are women overcoming lesbianism. I remember a class I conducted for a small group. I remarked to one sister in Christ, "Karen, you have such beautiful bone structure and pretty coloring!"

Her immediate reaction was to withdraw from me emotionally. Eyes narrowed, she watched me guardedly. "Oh, really?" was her only response.

I was not merely being effusive. Karen was very pretty. *What have I done to get such a reaction?* I wondered. In church a few days later, I asked, "Did I offend you somehow? It seemed as if suddenly you withdrew."

"Well, I did, in a way." Karen admitted. "One reason I ended up in lesbianism was that I was molested as a child by two older girls. The whole time they kept telling me how beautiful I was. I've just never wanted to be beautiful since."

Was it prejudice that caused me to think Karen's prettiness should be a source of pleasure to her? My perspective was so different. And, from her perspective, my view was all wrong. Karen's experience had taught her that being pretty was a bad thing; if she had been born ugly, she might not have been desirable and therefore might not have been sexually abused.

Sadly, many people who come for ministry have just such damaged concepts of life. God has invested in them a beautiful part of His creation, but sin has disfigured that creation. Rather than realizing the problem is sin, they blame the original creation. In fact, they even blame God. The rage we see in street demonstrations by militant gay rights activists is partly a manifestation of anger toward God for creating a life that seems incongruous to the experience of the owner.

The other side of this idea is that when someone comes to me for help, I may look at the outward creation and treat the person with complete disregard for their experience. That is what I did with Karen.

Karen and I have since become good friends. She has helped me to understand that even an attractive face can be the source of pain. For her, prettiness brought the negative attentions that led to brokenness in her sexual identity. But how could I learn to see things from other people's viewpoints? Their experiences and outlooks were so foreign to me!

Stumbling onto the Truth

The fire trail led up along a ridge. We cut off the main route and took a small path leading through scrub oak and poison oak. "Watch out!" I called back to my hiking partner. "This is all poison oak along here."

For years I had brought people into these hills near our home. Since not every hiker knew about poison oak, whenever I would pass this spot, I called back the same warning. Sylvia neatly sidestepped a branch and nodded in agreement. "Oh, yes," she smiled. "I'm quite familiar with poison oak. I used to get huge blisters on my hands from it."

We continued our hike along the ridge. The young woman beside me squinted when I asked, "What's going on with you and Corrine?"

"I feel so attracted to her," Sylvia confessed, beginning to cry. "I just want to be with her all the time."

I looked into her reddening eyes and shared my frustration with God.

Lord, why is Sylvia attracted to women? She's such a lovely girl—blonde, blue eyes, a pretty shape. And she's so nice! I know she loves You and wants to serve You. Why can't she straighten out this part of her life?

"Have you fallen together sexually?" I ventured. "Or are you just struggling with feelings?"

"It's just feelings, but ... I feel so helpless against the thoughts."

"You're right there—you are helpless," I said. "Listen, Sylvia, we can't fight such battles ourselves, no matter how commited we are. We have to give God complete authority in our lives. He can fight for you. He can win."

"Do you think I don't know that?" she spat out. "I've been struggling through this for two years now! I want to be free from these thoughts. People come back at me all the time with this stuff. Look, I know you mean well, but honestly, you don't know what it's like."

We walked along in chilly silence, each fighting our irritation.

Okay, Lord. I need your help here. What am I doing wrong?
I'm glad you asked.
You look at Sylvia's problems from the surface.
You see an attractive woman with a nice personality who loves Me.
To you that spells success.
But I see a hurt girl and the painful wounds she's endured.
Failure has been planted seed by seed throughout her life.
How can she reap success?
Well, what can we do? There has to be an answer.
Well, what is it?
We have to plant success?
Seed by seed.

"Sylvia?" I began anew. "Tell me about how you got here."
"How I got into the lifestyle and how I got to Love In Action?"
"Yeah."
"Well, my family was pretty normal." Her agitation seemed to be dissipating already. "I didn't have a bad childhood or anything. Things just went wrong later in my life."
"Your relationship with your mom was good?"
"Well, she'd get mad at me and yell a lot. I don't remember much about it. But I was always better friends with my dad."
Sometimes God graciously intervenes in a conversation like this. He who alone knows the complete truth can guide us to it. He did in this case. For at His prompting I asked the next question: "Sylvia, did your mother abuse you?"
"What? No, of course not. Well . . . oh, my . . ." Her stammering became less coherent as the tears began to fall. "I remember the neighbor coming to take me off our porch because my mom had locked me out. I was crying."
That simply and quickly, the truth dawned on Sylvia. Unbelievably, she had forgotten all about the years of verbal and emotional abuse at the hands of her mother. She eventually remembered more and more seeds for failure planted in her early life. Then, as we saw

some of the hurts and the lies behind them, we planned strategies to counteract them.

We would not have had any success if God had not intervened, however.

God's Heart for Healing

Lives already broken by sin—anyone's sin—fracture along lines we often cannot perceive. When hurting people try to repair their disrupted lives without God's help, they do a bad job.

The result is similar to a poorly set broken bone. From that point on, the life, like the bone, grows around the deformities. Everything about the bone—its shape, its use, the way it feels—is the result of adjusting to the deformity. Everything surrounding a broken life makes adjustments, too. Sometimes the result is a homosexual orientation.

In both cases a doctor needs to go in and fix the problem. However, there's only one Doctor who can fix a fractured life. Sometimes He uses assistants, but the ones who can be used first need to be trained.

Obviously, people who come to a cosmetics counter are not the same as those who come to our churches. But there are some parallels. The most important is this: The help we give should always be based on a Christlike response to *their* need rather than on *our* feelings and attitudes.

God inclines His heart toward hurting people. When they come into the church, we are like the doctor's assistants. Are we willing to learn how best to meet some of the special needs of these men and women? But unless we listen carefully to God's instructions and follow them to the letter, we will lose patients that could otherwise have been helped.

In my years of working with people who were formerly gay, I've learned many things. One important lesson is that we cannot just apply spiritual makeup, however holy we believe it to be. These men and women—our brothers and sisters in Christ—need some significantly deeper healing in their lives.

We can't tell an ex-lesbian to wear dresses and lipstick, and sooner or later her femininity will "click." Such new-found femininity may make *us* more comfortable, but it has nothing to do with making *her* more whole. The road to healing may take her through a lot more pain which we may not see or understand even if we did see. We dare not tell an "ex-gay" man that since he knows Jesus now, his sexual and relational desires will become more natural—just keep dating women. How can we, who do not know his struggles, possibly fathom God's timetable in healing them?

And we must not tell the hurting people who come into the church with sexual brokenness that theirs is the worst sin. Everyone's sin is the worst! It keeps them and us from fellowship with God, no matter what it is. There is nothing worse. The suffering people of God know it.

What kind of Christian are you? In what sort of church do you worship God? Whoever you are, God is calling upon you to share His heart of love and healing with a lost world. The luxury of bestowing His love according to our whim is nothing more than sinful self-indulgence.

The heart of God beat within the body of a man until, in one horrific moment, the pulse stopped and God, the man, died. When He arose from the dead, He invested in His servants the business of reaching others with the truth of His salvation. If you received Jesus as your Savior, the echo of His heartbeat for the wounded, lost, and bound should resound through your being. In Christ's name, how can we refuse to share His love with men and women seeking to overcome their homosexual past?

The harvest begins with me. The harvest begins with us.

In this book, we will examine the many practical facets of this rich harvest-in-the-making of men and women overcoming homosexuality. In chapters 11 and 12, Brad will detail a Christlike response to people infected with or affected by HIV/AIDS.

Instead of creating an unwanted harvest, we should join together and reap. Others have plowed and planted and watered. The

Lord of the harvest is watching expectantly. Our part is to gather in the bounty of God's abundant salvation to all people!

Chapter Two

The Elephant Men:
Real People Live Behind the Veils

"WHAT SHALL WE SAY THEN? SHALL WE CONTINUE IN SIN, THAT grace may abound? God forbid. How shall we, that are dead to sin, live any longer therein? Know ye not, that so many of us as were baptized into Jesus Christ were baptized into his death?"

The soft southern drawl spoke out suddenly from the congregation. A young man stood up, walked to the front of the church, and then faced us.

I was startled and perplexed as the next voice spoke: "Therefore we are buried with him by baptism into death: that like as Christ was raised up from the dead by the glory of the Father, even so we also should walk in newness of life." And he got up and walked to the front, standing beside the first man.

Is everyone supposed to know a verse, Lord? Is this something I missed in the announcements last week? I wondered.

A third man arose and spoke while standing in his place, his soft voice trembling with deep conviction. "For if we have been planted together in the likeness of his death, we shall be also in the likeness of his resurrection: Knowing this, that our old man is crucified with him, that the body of sin might be destroyed, that henceforth we should not serve sin. For he that is dead is freed from sin."

Oh, how can I be so dense? I thought, tears starting in my eyes. *Of course, this is Love In Action Night!*

Since the late 1970s, Love In Action has sponsored a live-in program for individuals seeking to make a break with their gay past and work toward emotional and relational healing. Most years, programs were only for men; several years there was a live-in for women. This time, it was men only.

Near the beginning of each year, the new program members and the live-in staff were introduced to our church fellowship. This evening's introduction took the form of the men's choral recitation of Romans 6.

"Now if we be dead with Christ, we believe that we shall also live with him." This man was less certain. He hesitated, then continued. "Knowing that Christ being raised from the dead dieth no more; death hath no more dominion over him." Sighing his relief, he walked to the front.

The familiar words spoken aloud in power and authority touched my heart deeply. All around, people were crying. Some were family members and close friends of those speaking. These brothers had come for healing! They were taking hard steps toward it, as one by one they spoke their portion and moved to join the men lined in front of the congregation.

"For in that he died, he died unto sin once: but in that he liveth, he liveth unto God . . ." *Likewise reckon ye also yourselves to be dead indeed unto sin.* I finished the next verse to myself as I recalled, *but alive unto God through Jesus Christ our Lord* (Rom. 6:1–11).

The Impact of One Man's Life

As I listened to the other men speak their parts, I began to recall faces of past members of this elite club—both men and women. Some had finished the live-in program and returned to homes scattered across the country and globe. Many had begun the healing process and were continuing their spiritual growth here. A few had died of AIDS. Some, tragically, had decided they could not "win through" and had gone back to the prison of a gay lifestyle.

Since its inception in 1973, Love In Action has been a turning point in the lives of hundreds of men and women working to overcome their broken gender identity and sexual orientation. Also founded in 1973, our church had grown and walked side by side with this ministry. Becoming an integral part of both organizations, the men and women of Love In Action were a rich segment of our church population.

Unsuspecting people often got a shock when they visited. I smiled in remembering the first time my father came to our church. We sat together at a Thanksgiving dinner service listening to our men's choir. Every man in the choir came from a gay background. As the music progressed, I sensed Daddy's perplexed look beside me. Finally, when the song stopped, I leaned over and asked, "Daddy, is something wrong?"

Uncomfortably he said, "Honey, I don't know how to tell you, but I think some of those young men might be gay."

I chuckled through my smile. "Well, they *all* were! Now they're all trying to leave homosexuality behind. I thought I'd told you about Love In Action, Daddy."

He sighed relief. "Oh, man, I thought you didn't know! When they got up and started singing, I got pretty worried."

Daddy's introduction to Love In Action at that Thanksgiving dinner was somewhat comical. But the following year, when Daddy was dying of lung cancer, he saw the serious side of the ministry. With only months left, he came to live with us. While in our home, one of those young men visited him faithfully. He shared the Lord and offered a friendly ear when my father needed to talk to someone other than family.

That dear brother—James—deserves some of the credit for Sol Stoumen's eventual salvation. My first experience with him was when he invited my husband, Mike, and me to come to his apartment for dinner. Though most pastors and their wives get such invitations, we rarely did.

James was hard for me to get used to. Even though we had dealt with "ex-gay" Christian men for ten years already, I was irritated by James' strong affectations, particularly in his speech. "Why can't he just talk like any other man?" I asked Mike as we drove home. "Does he know how *offensive* it is?"

"It wouldn't matter," he assured me. "James is changing. It just takes time. The longer the pattern of development, the more deeply ingrained the affectation. Some men will never entirely lose it."

"Are you sure he doesn't do it on purpose?" I persisted. "Are you sure he couldn't stop it if he wanted to?"

"I'm not sure of anything. But I have been told by those I trust. The affectations just take time to reverse."

Not everyone gets the time they need. James did. Mike and I watched him change into a new man. People like my father, who saw the changes from a worldly perspective, were amazed. Why?

A Matter of Right and Wrong

In recent years, every possible news media has presented supposedly "overwhelming evidence" that attempts to validate the born-gay-can't-change idea. Psychologists explain homosexuality as one of several different and yet "normal" lifestyle patterns into which a person's life may develop. Biomedical specialists search for proof of a genetic or hormonal basis for a homosexual orientation. Social philosophers seek new ethics to coincide with each new wave of moral change as it washes over a confused, misinformed world.

But regardless of the "evidence," men and women of conscience know the truth: Homosexual behaviors are contrary to the laws of God.

Satisfy every law and moral choice of *humans* and you still will have to deal with the law of *God*. We change our laws to fit the changes of our society. But the words of God cannot change because God Himself is immutable. That is why Jesus said, "Heaven and earth shall pass away: but my words shall not pass away" (Mark 13:31). God is the one true universal constant. He has never changed, nor will He ever.

Today's ideas and morals are completely different from those of my father's childhood. But the one remarkable and consistent fact is that God cares for us. This is truly wondrous and incredible, for we have no other significance.

We are so temporary upon this earth. The only thing that brings permanence to life is God's law planted and nurtured in a person's life. How can that happen? Both "the law" and "the word" are also used in reference to the man, Jesus Christ. To receive the Lord Jesus as Savior is to receive the Word of God into one's life. That does not mean getting a set of rules to live our lives by; rather we are given, by God's gracious intervention, a new life. The life of Jesus replaces our life. The man or woman who receives the Word—and thereby Jesus—will inherit eternal life. God's law brings us into right alignment with His plans and purposes. We become "right" with God.

If I am right with God, can I do whatever I want? No. Like the men in the live-in program were learning: "Let not sin therefore reign in your mortal body, that ye should obey it in the lusts thereof. Neither yield ye your members as instruments of unrighteousness unto sin: but yield yourselves unto God, as those that are alive from the dead, and your members as instruments of righteousness unto God" (Rom. 6:14–16).

When gays and lesbians become "right" with God, they begin to recognize that the opposite of right is wrong. Suddenly they are at ideological odds with the journalist, psychologist, geneticist, and sociologist. They know they have been told a lie and come to us, who know the truth, to learn.

What happens when men and women overcoming homosexuality come to our churches and homes for the truth? What happens when they turn away from that which is "wrong" and sin, and turn to that which is "right" and God's righteousness? Are we teaching them Romans 6:14–16 that sin has no dominion over them, that they are under grace and not law, and that they need not obey their old desires?

The Original Man Behind the Veil

In Victorian England there lived a man named John Merrick. Congenital deformities had so misshaped his head and body that the people of his time called him the "Elephant Man." Doomed to a horrid existence as a sideshow freak, he lived for years in poor health and depression.

Into this unfortunate man's life came a doctor. Though initially interested in him as a scientific curiousity, Dr. Treves eventually became John Merrick's friend.

The 1980 movie *The Elephant Man* vividly portrays the monstrous appearance of Mr. Merrick. And yet—more importantly, more poignantly—it also portrays the exquisite humanity imprisoned in that terrible body. Given the ability to look past his ugly exterior and into his heart, we find feelings so like our own. Here was a fine individual who knew the Bible and Book of Common Prayer well, but whose appearance excluded him from attending church.

Sadly, commoners in Merrick's day were unable to find charity for him. When forced to go out in public, Merrick wore a hat with a long curtain over his head to prevent his face being seen. It took support from influential people to afford him the simplest of lifestyles without constant harrassment.

Those on Both Sides of the Veil

The men and women who came to Church of the Open Door wanted to be obedient to God's Law. But they needed the help of His people. They wanted the support of a caring, committed group of Christians. They wanted a church which believed as they did that homosexuality was subject to Christ's healing and restoring authority—just as is every type of brokenness and orientation that deviates from God's design. In our church they found people with other kinds of wounds and sins willing to love them toward wholeness.

The brokenness of homosexuality does not happen overnight. Through a period of time and in response to a series of crises and decisions, people are deceived into following that course. Though God's reclamation takes place in the instant anyone asks for it, the outward evidence of that change may take a long time. Are we willing to work through the process of change with these children whom God loves?

God is not limited in His ability to change any of us. Instead, we are limited in our ability to respond to the new life we have received. But as we respond, change becomes evident. At first it may seem a small thing, but as we continue to walk in the right direction, more and more transformation occurs.

This is one of the most profound things I have seen in my twenty-plus years of ministry in this area: As more men and women have come to our church for healing in the area of sexual brokenness, our church as a ministering body has become more responsive to them.

Some people have left Open Door over the "ex-gay" issue, which may account for a greater overall degree of acceptance among those who remain. But, in fact, more people are getting involved in the lives of these men and women who have come out of their flawed pasts. We have become less judgmental and more forgiving about the affectations some have.

Most importantly, we have not yielded one bit on our stand that gays and lesbians need to renounce their sinful lifestyles and be healed by God. There has been compassion without compromise—not "pollution" in the church body, as some feared. And there has been healing—for the men and women who left homosexuality, as well as for us who previously allowed our zeal for God's Law, as we mistakenly saw it, to overthrow our obedience to His Word that we not judge one another.

Expectations, Time, and Change

Years ago a family joined our church straight out of the hippie movement. The wife, Sarah, was a thin, quick-minded sort who immediately plunged into the life of the church. She loved the fellowship and hungered to know Jesus better. About four months into her time at Open Door, Sarah got up to share a short, unplanned testimony at a women's luncheon.

We often had an open microphone at these meetings. The topic of the meeting was "Proper Household Management" or "Creating Memories on a Budget"—something along those lines in terms of eternal importance.

Sarah walked to the front. Her long, flowing skirt and wild, kinky hair punctuated each step. Wearing no makeup, sporting no manicure, her hiking boots sticking out incongruously beneath the skirt, she turned and smiled artlessly.

"I want to thank you all for the teaching today," she began. "It's going to take me some time to put the things I've heard into effect and I know I'll need some help and understanding.

"It's difficult to know how to be a Christian. Things are so very different from the life I've led. I only found out last week that I'm supposed to be wearing a bra! *Everyday!*"

Through the laughter we all saw the truth. We were placing requirements on this woman that God might not be making. We were asking her to conform to *our* image, not His. Although some conformity is necessary, we need to be careful that we focus upon those things which lead to life.

For most women and men, the process of overcoming homosexuality may take years. Many become discouraged. Often strong affectations and even stronger identification with their past sins remain evident in their lives. The men may be quite effeminate; the women, tough. These outward struggles and the even greater inward struggles work together to create an abyss where faith and trust can sink if they are not buoyed by the greater faith and trust of a church family. But, sadly, many fellow Christians look at former homosexuals and wonder why there are not greater outward changes.

Lifting the Veil

Sixteen men had come forward. Standing before us, in vulnerable humility, they declared the brokenness of homosexuality in their lives and asked our help in learning to overcome it.

Dear Lord, I've never had to confess my sins so publicly, I thought. *This takes incredible courage!*

John Smid, director of Love In Action, stepped to the microphone. "Ladies and gentlemen, I present to you the 1991 Love In Action Program. Each man will now give his name and where he is from." And they did.

"And now," John continued, "we'd like you church members to come forward, as you are led, and pray for these men. Take one of their cards and make a commitment to pray for them throughout this year's program."

Like a flood unleashed, people went forward and prayed for the men. I watched and waited for God to show me who to choose. By the end of the service I held three prayer cards.

In today's churches there are people who are badly disfigured and misunderstood, much like the Elephant Man. Having been ostracized so long for their spiritual deformity and sins, they learned to wear a covering. Sadly and too often, when those overcoming homosexuality remove theirs, they meet with judgment and prejudice rather than understanding and forgiveness.

Like John Merrick, the "ex-gay" members of our congregations want freedom from their damaging past. They want to be accepted for what they can be, rather than judged for what they have been. They desperately need someone to look beyond the ugliness of past sin in their lives and see God's image which He created there. We cannot help until we develop the Lord's perspective—one of compassion without compromise.

CHAPTER THREE

Wheat and Tares: The Biblical View of Sexuality and Homosexuality

EVERY YEAR IN THE CENTRAL VALLEY OF NORTHERN CALIFORNIA, rice farmers flood their fields and drop the seed from planes. As the rice grows to what one farmer's wife calls the "golf course" stage—bright green blades carpeting the water—another plant often emerges.

Water grass is a vigorous weed flourishing under the same conditions as rice. This pest crop reseeds itself from year to year, with seeds staying in the rice fields but not always showing up in successive seasons. In its early stage, the weed looks so similar to rice, most people would not notice it.

If detection is difficult, eradication is more so. Applied by air, weed killers are expensive and often ineffective. And, as water grass grows, its more vigorous growth pattern causes it to tower over and shade the developing rice. This competition naturally affects the productivity of the field.

The weed cannot be removed during harvest either. Water grass "shells out" earlier than rice; by rice harvest time, it has already reseeded with seeds too small for harvesters to pick up.

Obviously, a farmer's choice would be to begin with a field completely free of all contaminants, apply pure seed, and maintain equally pure growing conditions. However, since the Fall of man, farmers have not had that opportunity.

Similar to California's farmers, those of us who toil in the Lords' fields often confront conditions which hamper our best efforts. Each year we work to raise up to God's glory a crop of men and women who are fruitful and bring increase to His kingdom. And each year we see contaminants that detract from the work and weaken ministry effectiveness.

Nor do we see the same pattern from year to year. Because people often judge their lives by a constantly shifting set of values rather than God's Word, they end up nearer or farther from God's plan in the process. How can we be certain that the field we plant conforms to His guidelines so that the harvest we produce meets with His approval?

Using the Right Guidelines

Can you imagine farmers trying to grow rice without properly preparing their fields? Or planting without regard to the best growing conditions? Do you think they would produce enough to make their living? Naturally not! Crops would fail and farmers would be out of business.

Why then do so many Christian workers attempt to produce a crop in the field of the Lord without paying careful attention to every aspect of His instructions as detailed in the Bible? Do we think we know more today than our Creator? Do we believe the Bible has lost its effectiveness?

I believe the Bible is the complete, accurate, and inerrant Word of God and that God inspired every word—including, as one beloved pastor used to say, "the cover. It says Holy and that's what it is." Each controversy in our lives, when measured against the perfect standard of God's Holy Bible, is solvable (see 2 Tim. 3:16.)

The Holy Spirit's job is to use God's Word to teach us what is necessary. We need not be scholars in Greek or Hebrew to understand what God has said. That is not to say additional books would not provide greater insight; they do, and I use all kinds of tools when I study the Bible. But you do not have to be a great intellectual to understand it, nor do you require special training. God meant for His children to understand His instructions. So, for the most part, they are pretty straightforward.

What about "new" teachings? What about new information from secular and Christian scholars? Should we judge what we know of Scripture against what we continue to learn about ourselves and our environment?

Let us be very clear: Any teaching which contradicts Scripture should be discarded. It really does not matter how well-lettered and prestigious the teachers—if what they teach fails to align with the whole Bible, it is not the truth.

Much of pro-gay teaching regarding homosexuality in Scripture comes by just such a circuitous route. New teachings which pervert the meaning and intent of Scripture are really old snakes who have shed their skins to blend in better. Their bite is still as lethal. Watch out!

The Need for Companionship

"And the LORD God said, It is not good that the man should be alone; I will make him an help meet for him" (Gen. 2:18). God had just finished creating all of the world. With each new addition, God said it was good. Now, after creating the man, God said something was *not* good. The man should not be alone. So God created all the animals of the earth and brought them to the man to name. As wondrous and incredible as they were, still none among the animals could be a companion to bring completion to the man.

So God fashioned woman out of one of the man's ribs. Now the man was satisfied. He had the one companion who fit him and his needs: "Therefore shall a man leave his father and his mother, and shall cleave unto his wife: and they shall be one flesh" (Gen. 2:24).

God's original design for man was that he would live with the woman (one woman obviously, as there was only one) and that they would become one flesh. God instructed the people to be fruitful and multiply—to have children. God designed our sexuality for reproduction and for pleasure. His intent from the very beginning was clearly for sexual intimacy to be expressed between a man and a woman.

From Genesis to Revelation, the commandments of the Lord can be traced. The pattern is the same: A man is to marry a woman, and there must not be sexual experience outside marriage. God's intent has not changed since the Creation. Likewise, His design for our lives is to be married to one member of the opposite sex, or to be sexually abstinent if unmarried. Read through the Bible and look at couples there whose lives are blessed. This pattern is plain.

Critiquing Pro-Gay Theology

Where did homosexuality come in? Did everything change after the Fall? Did homosexual activity become acceptable then?

There are two ways to know what God wants regarding anything questionable. You can look at what God says, just as above. And you can also look at what God does *not* say. *Nowhere* in Scripture does God bless sexual union between members of the same sex. *Nowhere* is homosexual behavior of any kind called acceptable. If so-called "homosexual unions" were good, wouldn't God have told us so? On the other hand, there are several instances where God speaks plainly against both homosexuality in men and lesbianism in women.

In recent years, some passages of Scripture have been under dispute as to both content (what they say) and intent (what they mean). As you read, think of each passage within the context of the whole Bible and the purity of God. What is God saying? And what is He *not* saying?

The first passage of Scripture is Genesis 19. Beginning in the first verse of this chapter we learn that two angels came to the wicked city of Sodom where Abraham's nephew, Lot, lived. The angels said they would sleep in the street all night, but Lot entreated them to be his guests. That evening the men of the city came and, surrounding the house, demanded that Lot send his guests out to them. Why? "Bring them out unto us that we may know them" (v. 5).

These were not neighbors trying to be sociable to strangers. They wanted to rape these two men. How can we be sure that is the case? We could look to the original Hebrew, and discover that this was the same kind of "knowing" where Adam knew Eve his wife before she conceived Cain (Gen. 4:1). But we might also see in Genesis 19 that Lot offered his two virgin daughters to the men as substitutes for the angels.

Pro-gay theologians attempt to teach from Scripture that God acccepts homosexuality. Some of these teachers have identified themselves as being gay; others are straight. Either way, their theology is "gay affirmative"—it supports and promotes "loving" (as opposed to abusive) homosexual relationships as acceptable, achievable, and admirable.

Using part of Ezekiel 16:49, pro-gay theologians claim the real sins in Sodom were not homosexual activity, but lack of hospitality and care for the poor. Or that the problem in Genesis 19 was the men were going to take these angels by force. In other words, it would have been all right if the angels had been consenting. If, as these pro-gay teachers say, the sin was not mere homosexual activity but rape, the passage might not apply to everyone living the gay lifestyle today.

Hmm. Read both of these passages for yourself. What do you think? Your answer is important because if you believe homosexual behavior in any form is okay, you certainly would not be able to help those desiring change.

The passage does apply. Scripture always is in agreement with itself and same-sex activity is specifically prohibited in other places. From Genesis onward, Sodomites are mentioned several times, *always* with a strong indictment from God against them and sometimes specifically mentioning sexual perversion (see Jude 7).

Who or What Is an "Abomination"?

Leviticus 18 and 20 both deal with very similar subject matter. Chapter 18 is about incest: "None of you shall approach to any that is near of kin to him, to uncover their nakedness: I am the LORD" (v. 6).

Following this initial statement are numerous possible situations of incestuous relations with women. Obviously, God was speaking to men here, as He said, "none . . . shall approach . . . any near of kin to *him* . . ." [emphasis added]. After all relationships with kinswomen are listed, the Lord mentioned several other possibilities of sexual sin or causes for "ceremonial uncleanness." Verse 19 warns against intercourse with a menstruating woman; verse 20 says not to lie with your neighbor's wife. Verse 21 commands that children were not to be offered in sacrifice to the god Molech, and verse 22 says: "Thou shalt not lie with mankind, as with womankind: *it* is abomination" [emphasis added].

This is pretty simple! No Hebrew to read. It's plain what God is saying. It is *wrong* in our Creator's sight for a man to have sexual relations with another man. Note also God *does not condemn the individuals* as being abominations to Him, but their *actions*. This is even more clear in Leviticus 20:13:

"If a man also lieth with mankind, as he lieth with a woman, both of them have *committed* an abomination: they shall surely be put to death; their blood shall be upon them" [emphasis added].

Many pro-gay theologians use the argument today that these Old Testament restrictions are not required of those who live under grace. Of course, using that same logic, sex with animals—prohibited in the Mosaic Law—would now be acceptable under the age of grace.[1]

Jesus said, "I am come not to destroy [the law] but to fulfill [it]" (Matt. 5:17). The New Testament relationship we enjoy with the Lord should never be an excuse for greater sin, but rather the reason for greater sanctification.

What Is "Natural"?

Countering those who say Old Testament restrictions no longer apply, we do have New Testament guidelines that explicitly forbid homosexual involvement. And Paul in Romans noted lesbian sex also is contrary to God's intent: "For this cause God gave them up into vile affections: for even their women did change the natural use into that which is against nature: And likewise also the men, leaving the natural use of the woman, burned in their lust one toward another; men with men working that which is unseemly; and receiving in themselves that recompense of their error which was meet" (Rom. 1:26–27).

What did Paul mean by "natural"? Pro-gay theologians claim that some men and women are born homosexual. Therefore, a homosexual orientation is "natural" to them. By acting upon their homosexual "nature," they have not changed what is natural. Further, they argue that other people are truly heterosexual but change to homosexual behavior for some reason; only these acts can be considered sinful because they go against "nature" for the heterosexual person.

Read the passage again. Let the Holy Spirit speak to your heart as you read it. Is that interpretation what this passage really says and means?

These verses from Romans contain within them the very rebuttal to the "natural" argument. Paul clearly states that it is natural for a man to have intercourse with a woman. He did not say, as he might have, "the women did change the natural use into that which is against *their* nature." Rather, he said what they are doing is *against nature*, i.e., against God's intent. Paul, who often went to almost endless explanation to clearly define what he meant, certainly could have clarified this matter if he did not rightly believe he had stated the obvious quite succinctly.

In addition, if homosexuality were a natural state to some, as is taught today, why would Paul state plainly that the effeminate (1 Cor. 6:9) would not inherit the kingdom of God? Why did he link them in a group and label the group as unrighteous? "Know ye not that the unrighteous shall not inherit the kingdom of God? Be not deceived: neither fornicators, nor idolaters, nor adulterers, nor effeminate, nor abusers of themselves with mankind [i.e., homosexuals], nor thieves, nor covetous, nor drunkards, nor revilers, nor extortioners, shall inherit the kingdom of God" (1 Cor. 6:9–10).

But it is also clear in the same passage that some believers at Corinth had come from a homosexual background—which gives us evidence that transformation is possible: "And such were some of you: but ye are washed, but ye are sanctified, but ye are justified in the name of the Lord Jesus, and by the Spirit of God" (1 Cor. 6:11).

Finally, perhaps the best practical argument refuting the notion that God created some to be natural as gays or lesbians comes from John Smid of Love In Action. Quite simply he states, "The parts just don't fit. I tried it for four years and I can tell you. The parts don't fit." Pretty obvious. God is quite ingenious. If He had planned for men and women to be physically intimate with the same sex, would He not have designed us that way? But He didn't because He never intended for us to have homosexual relationships.

Wheat and Tares

In the past thirty years, the world has chosen to redefine morality to fit the "newer" standards of the "now" generation, rather than accepting the truth of Scripture and the sovereignty of God. A new breed of theologians, hiding under the guise of compassion and truth, distorts the Word of God in an attempt to justify a sin they or others refuse to give up.

We must be charitable: Some of these theologians are truly Christians, just deluded by whatever motivates them; others may not be. Regardless, their influence has grown. How can this be? Is the church not the Body of Christ?

Jesus taught on this subject one day as recorded in Matthew 13. His parable about a wheat crop infested with weeds parallels California's rice and water grass problem. Though the farmer sowed good seed, an enemy came and sowed tares in the field. When the grain grew, he knew that the tares were the work of an enemy. But he would not let his servants uproot the weeds for fear of harming the good grain.

He said, "Let both grow together until the harvest: and in the time of harvest I will say to the reapers, 'Gather ye together first the tares, and bind them in bundles to burn them: but gather the wheat into my barn' " (Matt. 13:30).

The disciples did not understand, so He explained: "He that soweth the good seed is the Son of Man; the field is the world; the good seed are the children of the kingdom; but the tares are the children of the wicked one; the enemy that sowed them is the devil; . . . and the reapers are the angels. As therefore the tares are gathered and burned in the fire; so shall it be in the end of this world" (Matt. 13:37b–40).

Within His field, some will grow along with the good wheat of God, looking like it in many ways and even rooted with it. However, they will not be real wheat, but counterfeits whose true identity will become known in time. In the end, the Lord's angels will gather them into bundles and cast them into the fire. These are the same ones to whom Jesus will say, "I never knew you: depart from me ye that work iniquity " (Matt. 7:23).

And what about the good wheat? What can the wheat do about the tares? The most important thing the good wheat can do is raise up the crop it was planted for. The job of the wheat is not to try to uproot the tares. Likewise, we who know the truth are not called to try to uproot those theologians or churches which teach lies. Instead, we must continue to teach the truth from the Word of God, producing as much fruit as we can. And we must grow vigorously ourselves to successfully compete with the weeds growing around us.

Pro-gay theologians make many other specific points in their attempts to win the case for general acceptance of homosexual behaviors. Many points require subtle and disturbing twists of Scriptures to try to convert people to an unrighteous view. If these concern you, contact Exodus International (see resource section.)

CHAPTER FOUR

The Way He Should Go:
God's Design for Gender Identity

THE WINDING ROAD LEADS UPWARD THROUGH THE DENSE GROWTH
where Ponderosa pine gradually gives way to Douglas fir. As you
climb, the air becomes cooler and thinner; the sunlight, more
dappled. Somewhere along Trail Ridge Road in Rocky Mountain
National Park, mountain meadows and montane forests are replaced by the subalpine forests that skirt the sides of the giant
mountain peaks forming the Continental Divide.

Here in the subalpine forest, Engelmann spruce and subalpine
fir grow amidst the lush greenery. Hundreds of wildflowers dot the
emerald enclosures where, at every turn of the trail, water runs
through tiny canyons to the valley floor.

Spruce and fir of subalpine forests grow to heights of 130 feet
and 100 feet respectively in this rich and encouraging environment
between about 9,000 and 11,500 feet elevation. But at the upper
edge of this abundant growth is a thin line of demarcation—a
miniature forest of scarred and twisted trees called *krummholz*
(German for "crooked wood"). The same trees which grow so
hardily in the subalpine forest, here at the tree line may only reach
a few feet high, though they are centuries old. They ought to kiss
the sky with lush green branches; instead, they barely hit my waist!

These dwarfed trees are not growing as they should. Branches
venture out only on the side opposite the strong winds or com-

37

pletely flatten out over the ground like a bush to avoid the wind. The exposed bark is scarred by blowing sand and snow. These factors, plus bitter cold and an inadequate water supply, combine to batter the tiny forest whose survival depends upon adaptation to its harsh world.

Like little old men and women, these contorted little trees push to the outer edge of their own limitations. Trying to live in a world where they do not belong, they may survive, but they cannot thrive.

I see a parallel between these *krummholz* and the men and women who live a life immersed in homosexuality. They do not achieve the fullness of their heterosexual counterparts, despite denials and protestations to the contrary. Though I have known many homosexual people who were successful on one level, I have never known any whose lives were well-rounded.

Is the lack of blessing in the experience of self-identified gays and lesbians merely the result of unfair treatment and prejudice from the heterosexual community? Or is it something more? Are they, like the dwarfed trees above the tree line, trying to exist in a niche where God never intended them to be? Clearly, they are not growing as they should.

How did they get there? How did these people whom God loves find themselves in such a forbidding soil?

In this chapter we will look at God's original design for men and women—in other words, "the way they should go," as we see in Proverbs 22:6: "Train up a child in the way he should go: and when he is old, he will not depart from it."

We will also examine how God's design became broken and distorted, and some of the basic lures to homosexuality that may result. As simplified as these explanations seem, they become as intricate, unique, and complex as the varied lives of the women and men to whom they apply.

There is no simple formula for causes of homosexuality, just as there are no quick fixes. However, keys to causes can be found—and offer hope for solutions—in the following:

+ Our relationship with God

- ✦ Masculinity, femininity, and gender identity as God designed it
- ✦ Our relationship with our unique self
- ✦ Stable and safe family environment
- ✦ Parent/child relationships
- ✦ Community relations
- ✦ Peers and friendships
- ✦ Sexual and sexuality development
- ✦ Adult sexual and subcultural involvement

As you can see, most of these deal with relationships. In fact, it would seem that a homosexual orientation is based on emotional and relational problems.

At every point, God wants to intervene and show us the blessing He intends to make in each of these nine areas. In each crucial relationship lies the opportunity for people struggling with homosexuality to allow God's best.

We will look at each relationship or issue, first as God meant things to be for us, then as it has become through our brokenness, and finally as to the harvest which may result in our lives. (I use *we, ours,* and *us* here because these principles of God's design apply universally, though our particular brokenness may not turn toward homosexuality.) Other chapters will present numerous personal examples of these root issues, taken from Christian men and women who have exited a gay or lesbian lifestyle.

Our Relationship with God

God's plan in creating us was that we would perceive ourselves based upon an intimate understanding of our Maker and His love for us. God wants to relate with us personally and have us know Him personally. Thus, from Him we derive our worth. We see the outworking of God's desire to fellowship with His creatures in the way Jesus reached out and responded to men and women while on earth.

Humanity's brokenness in sin brought separation from God and therefore a loss of intimacy. We did not know our Lord anymore, so how could we know where we stood with Him? The assurance of His love and approval were lost. With that, the confidence of our place in His creation disappeared.

Sin, left unchecked, damages us and restructures our identity. Rather than having the intended outcome of a close friendship with God, our lives are spent trying to achieve His approval, never knowing how much He loves us. We are outsiders of the kingdom rather than intimates of the court.

Masculinity, Femininity, and Gender Identity

Understanding gender is one of the most important keys to transformation. And to say merely that "men are supposed to initiate and women are supposed to respond" is a gross oversimplification of a complex relational issue.

The first three chapters of Genesis show us what God designed men and women to be and to do. Let's take a look at those chapters.

Although God created all people in His image, He built in some differences between the sexes. Simply stated, men and women are not exactly alike; that is called *polarity*. In fact, these differences are profound, though *complementary*. As Brad says when he teaches on gender issues, "They were made to complete—not compete." God designed men and women to work together as a true team to build up His kingdom. Sin brings in competition and conflict between the genders.

God designed men to be strongly involved in their world and take initiative in subduing the earth. His plan was that men lead through sensitive, tender involvement with others, giving themselves fully to make an impact. God put Adam in the midst of the Garden to keep and till it, and ever since men seem to be focused more on their work than anything else. (The word *keep* in the Hebrew gives a picture of cutting a swath through the vegetation—organizing and shaping it.)

God designed women to be strong of character, strong in supporting others, and vulnerable—to be impacted and to impact through relationships with others. God put Eve with Adam as a helpmate. *Helpmate* itself implies assistance. Woman was originally created to excel in supporting roles.

Both of these roles are necessary and good; brokenness came in because both the man and woman disobeyed God: "And when the woman saw that the tree was good for food, and that it was pleasant to the eyes, and a tree to be desired to make one wise, she took of the fruit thereof, and did eat, and gave also unto her husband *with her,* and he did eat" (Gen. 3:6, emphasis added).

Though Eve was deceived by the serpent, the original Hebrew makes it clear that *Adam was right there with Eve* during her decision to eat of the forbidden fruit, and her first bites into it.

It is interesting that the curses God handed down parallel His original design. Now the man would have great difficulty subduing his world, because God cursed the ground. Now the woman would have great difficulty in her role of completing the man and supporting him. She would have pain in childbirth and *desire* to rule over her husband. (The same Hebrew word used in Genesis 3:16 of the woman's *desire* being toward her husband is used in Genesis 4:7 of sin crouching at Cain's door, *desiring to rule over him.*)

In addition, as a result of the Fall, both men and women have self-protective strategies as part of their nature. Men fear taking the initiative and being sensitive in relationships. Why? They desire affirmation and respect, but they also fear being exposed as inadequate, incompetent, and unable to make an impact in their world and relationships. So they tend to passively avoid situations that put them at risk of exposure. Passivity is men's biggest problem.

Women fear being vulnerable, of opening themselves to others in relationships. Why? They desire love and acceptance, but they also fear being abused, rejected, and having such little value that someone would choose not to enter their lives. So they tend to control situations that put themselves at risk of rejection. Control is women's biggest problem.

Often, we will see almost a caricature of these two problems within the gay and lesbian communities, as well as among those trying to exit it. If straight men are passive, gay men tend to be even more so. If straight women are controlling, lesbian women tend to be more so. Granted, these are stereotypes. But, in this case, there is more than a grain of truth to them. That is why, in part, the transformation process takes time; there is a lot in their gender identities to transform!

But what exactly is gender identity? Far beyond just stereotypical roles and behaviors, it is the heart-level alliance one feels (or does not feel) with his or her God-given gender. Boys should grow up feeling masculine—that they fit in with other boys and men. Girls should grow up feeling feminine—that they fit in with other girls and women. However, sometimes these internal allegiances get crossed, especially for those who end up with homosexual feelings: Boys often feel more allied with women, femininity, and women's culturally defined roles; girls often feel more allied with men, masculinity, and men's culturally defined roles. They do not identify with their God-ordained gender.

For former gays and lesbians, reclaiming their true gender identity as a man or woman is often traumatic, yet transforming. When Brad teaches on this subject, he uses this illustration: Healing is like checking into a hotel. When former gays and lesbians choose to realign themselves with their God-given masculinity or femininity (often despite not *feeling* it), they have finally gotten off the elevator and entered into the hallway of healing. Once inside, they may be surprised to find myriads of other men and women from all kinds of broken backgrounds similarly seeking their rooms. No one cares any longer where anyone's emotional baggage came from; the key thing is that everyone is now in the hallway of healing. Those who have found healing before now serve as bellhops to point the way to rooms of rest and restoration.

Our Relationship with Our Unique Self

Next to our relationship with God, our most important alliance is the one we make with ourselves in our God-planned uniqueness. The Lord knew everything about us from the moment He fashioned us individually, including the most minute attributes of our makeup. His purpose in weaving such diversity among us was that we should each enjoy a special position in the creation. Thus, we derive confidence in who God created us to be. Like the trees in the heart of the subalpine region, we should be reaching upward to the heights of what He has created in us.

The Fall brought all attributes of our personhood under the dominion of a fallen nature. God intended every aspect of our character, appearance, family background, monetary status, etc., for our good. But we don't see His purpose when we look for the world's blessing and not at our relationship with a loving God. Instead, we filter everything about who we are through the broken mirror of worldly standards.

In addition, others may notice different and vulnerable areas of our lives—like our above- or below-average looks, intelligence, athletic abilities, family's social status. These peculiarities, however, are part of the unique creation God intended. But judged through the eyes of an often hostile world, our uniqueness may engender teasing and taunting. Sadly, some of our most special attributes end up being the cause of isolation from others.

There is nothing we can do about what others think of us. But contrary to the familiar childhood taunt of "Sticks and stones . . . names *do* hurt if we begin to identify ourselves with them and label ourselves with false attributes. Children who do so may never be able to break the hold that a negative nickname has over their lives.

Dissatisfaction with the unique individual we were created to be results. We are not happy or fulfilled in our personhood. Somehow God's incredible workmanship is judged and found wanting. Not measuring up, we strive to conform in an effort to recreate ourselves in the world's image.

It is a wicked progression. By the time we mature we have abandoned the person God blessed us to be. We have instead embraced the person those around us believe or want us to be—so we can please them. We fall victim to the judgment of a heartless and unloving world. The feeling of being different or deficient develops the core of a false, insecure identity as we begin to believe the labels others place on us, rather than the promises of God for our lives.

Stable and Safe Family Environment

God designed the family as a place of safety and security, dependent upon a strong marriage between a man and woman whose lives are submitted to Him. Our understanding of ourselves and our world should be based upon a loving environment within a godly family. Masculine and feminine gender identity should have been incorporated into our being via bonding with and learning from both of our parents. Also, the ravages of the world around us *should* be repaired in the comfort of our homes. For most of us, none of these have been our full experience.

Sin results in family dysfunction. *Dysfunction* really means, "the results of sin and/or trauma which cause relational breakdown and improper workings of the family." In short, the family structure does not work, and the intended security and safety for its members do not happen.

Some sin-related causes of family dysfunction are:

+ Addictive behaviors, such as gambling, compulsive shopping sprees, or driving recklessly
+ Sexual addictions, such as viewing pornography, visiting prostitutes, or exhibitionism
+ Physical addictions, such as to alcohol, food, or prescription or illegal drugs
+ Various forms of abuse, such as emotional, physical, sexual, verbal, or neglect

+ Any other kind of rebellion against God or idolatry, such as occult involvement, criminal activity, or even humanistic do-goodism that leaves God out.

In fact, almost any sin can be the basis of family troubles.

What constitutes a trauma? Anything that promotes a sense of being rejected, abandoned, abused, or vulnerable. Whether real or only in the perception of the child, traumas can cause damage. Sometimes a trauma exists over a short period, but its conse-quences last a long time. The key is in how a child perceives the event(s). These are some trauma-related causes of dysfunction in families:

+ Death in the family

+ Physical or mental illness

+ Separation or abandonment, such as by divorce, or a parent going off to war, away on business, or even on a vacation without the children

+ Natural disasters or other major disruptive events, such as earthquakes, fires, or a car accident. Even a geographical relo-cation with ensuing culture shock can be the source of trauma.

Whatever the source, dysfunction may result in the breakdown of appropriate family relations and the building up of inappropri-ate interactions in their place. Something other than a strong husband/wife marital bond becomes the focal point for the family's interaction.

Parent/Child Relationships

Because masculinity and femininity are attitudes and character qualities role modeled by parents, the most important relationship to the development of healthy gender identity is the child's rela-tionship to the same-sex parent.

If parental dysfunction is hindering the child's ability to bond with their same-sex parent, gender identity confusion and/or re-jection may result. In other words, children may feel ambivalent about their gender or they may decide they do not want to be as they were created. They may cross-identify themselves with the opposite sex instead.

Masculine and feminine qualities are also "called forth" from the child by the same-sex parent. This is especially true during the adolescent transition into adulthood, when parents affirm the manliness of their near-adult sons and the womanliness of their near-adult daughters. For instance, fathers can teach their sons the fine art of shaving. Mothers can teach their daughters about menstruation and help them when their first period arrives. These rites of passage in our culture signify a child is now moving into adulthood. They should be joyous times with an appropriate amount of fuss.

Sadly, a parent's own brokenness and lack of affirmation in their own gender often causes a breakdown in their relationship with a same-sex child and in their ability to affirm their children.

Next in importance is the child's relationship with their opposite-sex parent. Two questions I hear asked frequently are: Do gay men always descend from dominating mothers? Do lesbians always develop from little girls whose fathers wanted sons instead? My basic answer to both questions is *no*. Although there may be an element of truth in each, these are vast oversimplifications of a complex set of root problems. Take, for instance, the case of a boy whose father is physically or emotionally absent. The father's absence creates a vacuum, and generally the mother steps into that gap. She may be sincere, appear domineering, or may actually be domineering—but the main problem is still the boy missing his father. No woman can fill the "father hunger" in her son's soul. The lack of his presence potentially sets the son up to identify with women by default.

Similarly, if a girl loves rough-and-tumble games and turns into a "tomboy," a father who encourages those things can reinforce patterns consistent with later lesbianism. But I would say that the stronger underlying problem is the girl's lack of identification with girls and women, usually promoted by a strained relationship with her mother. Thus, the father's influence is by default.

No one has a perfect formula for raising children who are totally healthy in their sexuality. And in our brokenness, we do not know at times how to go about parenting properly.

Worse, our ineptitude in parenting often means we fail to produce a home which encourages love and mutual respect among our children, their siblings, and other significant extended family members. As a result, children may fall prey to dangers both outside our homes and within. These include: incest, rape, sexual abuse, sibling rivalry, and rebellion against parental authority. All of these, as well as other related family problems are the result of brokenness.

And what is the result of poor family relations? Children with an unstable family life feel insecure in their sense of being—of self, identity, and personhood. Also, as mentioned before, they may be insecure in their sense of gender identity and feel like outsiders among members of their own sex.

Though gender identity confusion is not the only possible result of familial dysfunction, and the broken parent/child relationships that result from it, it is very often present. Boys will feel they do not fit in the world of boys and men; girls will feel they do not fit in with girls and women. Neither will believe they are as they should be, or as everyone else is.

When children become insecure in this area, their blocked, God-given longing to enter fully into their gender identity may begin to express itself in longings to bond with a substitute parent or to find some substance or activity to numb the emotional pain. Carried to its fullest extent, this longing may result in the brokenness of a homosexual orientation and the sin of homosexual behavior.

Community Relations

God designed His creation to work together in harmony. The larger community should provide solid and secure relationships to augment those of the family unit. Older women should teach and mentor younger women and girls, encouraging them in feminine character and strength. Older men should teach and mentor younger men and boys, promoting masculine vision and responsibility.

But our communities are not what they once were. Various factors, including urbanization (we tend to live in large communities where we neither know nor are we known), greater mobility (we move more than before), and the breakdown of traditional strengths within our ethnic backgrounds all combine to undermine what might otherwise be an effective network of help for young men and women.

This means a child has even fewer community-based relationships to draw upon when entering his/her adolescent and adult years. There simply are no supporting individuals to call positive attention to emerging manhood or womanhood, and thereby strengthen a young man's or woman's sense of belonging to his/her gender. Instead of having their gender affirmed and reinforced, young people are abandoned to their own resources or to those wishing to exploit gender confusion and vulnerabilities for evil purposes.

Peers and Friendships

God designed friendships to provide comfort and help in this world. We should experience a degree of intimacy with a small circle of friends. Early friendships tend to be with members of the same sex. During puberty, these same-sex huddles break up as boys begin to notice girls, and girls begin to pay attention to boys.

Children who have not had healthy relating with their same-sex parent or surrogate and who thus approach adolescence with a severe deficit in same-sex bonding, may continue to seek the intimacy they were denied. Instead of moving into alliances with the opposite sex, these young men and women often find themselves left behind while their peers go forward. This increases both the sense of alienation in these young people and their neediness for emotionally satisfying/intimate friendships with members of the same sex.

Sexual and Sexuality Development

In addition, physical characteristics begin to be a major focus for adolescents as they enter puberty. This sexual development may prove another source of confusion and embarrassment for those already inclined by other factors toward same-sex *emotional* feelings. Now, in the flood of sex hormones, these emotional feelings turn *erotic.*

Further, children and adolescents may fall victim to various kinds of sexual trauma. These might include sexual abuse, incest, rape, emotional incest, and sexual experimentation. (Emotional incest occurs when a parent treats a child of either gender as a substitute spouse when a real spouse is physically or emotionally absent from the marriage relationship. This places adult expectations and responsibilites on the child—something he or she was not designed to bear.)

Current estimates are that one in every three girls alive in the United States today will be the victim of sexual abuse by age 18, as will one in every four boys. Approximately half of these will be incest victims, i.e., sexually used by a parent, significantly older sibling, or caretaker.

By *very* conservative estimates, 80 percent of Christian women working to overcome lesbianism have been victims of sexual abuse, incest, or rape. For Christian men overcoming homosexuality, one 1989 study found 35 percent were victims of sexual abuse. However, the actual percentages for men may well be higher, perhaps just as high as for women. Why? Only since the mid-1980s have men been able to define what happened to them as actually constituting sexual abuse.

A homosexual orientation develops through a series of steps. First comes a child's sense of feeling different. He or she is an outsider within his or her own gender, experiencing gender confusion or an insecure gender identity. Then, generally, a lack of bonding continues with the same-sex parent, resulting in strong emotional needs for affirmation and friendship from members of the same sex. With puberty, this homo-emotional need transmutates into homosexual desires. And any sexual experimentation or sexual abuse prematurely engages the erotic nature.

Like little trees which cannot grow taller because of the poor conditions under which they struggle, children who grow up with serious emotional deficits and crippling relational disadvantages do not thrive. What homosexually inclined young people need is to fill the emotional void in their lives with legitimate relational intimacy. But they do not know how to develop intimate friendships, and often equate physical expressions of sexuality with relational intimacy. In short, they long for intimacy, but they learn to settle for sex. At this point positive and safe relationships with same-sex adults can offer the most help for struggling adolescents (see chap. 7).

Adult Sexual and Subcultural Involvement

God's design for sexuality is clear in the Bible. We must either live as partners in an intact marriage with a member of the opposite sex or abstain from sexual relations.

In the Bible, fornication (sexual intercourse between two unmarried people), adultery (intercourse where one person is married to someone else), and homosexual involvement are *never* condoned or spoken of as acceptable in God's sight.

The unmet legitimate desire for same-sex relational intimacy (i.e., a strong, safe, and normal friendship) becomes an illegitimate desire for sexual intimacy. Some are able to say no to homosexual involvement. Many do not, and feelings turn into actions.

Homosexual activities can range from encounters with anonymous partners, to "monogamous" relationships, to sexual addiction accompanied by high levels of promiscuous behavior, to no interpersonal involvement but a strong fantasy life, to addiction to pornography. Some succumb to emotional dependency—a state of substantial personal and emotional entanglement between two people, regardless of whether they are sexually involved with each other.

The resulting damage in men and women who are homosexually oriented depends somewhat on the level of their sexual involvement. If they abstain from actual activity, they will most likely retain a semblance of innocence. Once a person becomes actively involved in homosexual behavior, however, the effects of their sin—like those of any ungodly sexual involvement—create lasting and often devastating consequences: loss of innocence, heightened eroticism, flashbacks to past sexual encounters, and so forth.

One of the most far-reaching results is that many (though not all) people involved with homosexuality accept a new identity—being gay. What is the difference between dealing with homosexual feelings and being gay? Becoming gay is a step beyond a homosexual orientation into a changed lifestyle: entering a multifaceted alternative subculture that entails choices in the personal, relational, political, social, and economic realms.

Gays and lesbians may create a "family of choice" by developing a support network of other gay individuals. They have their own political action groups, social clubs, vacation spots, products, services, and stores. There are pro-gay theologies and gay committees within religious denominations—even a gay denomination itself (the Metropolitan Community Church). Also, there are various sub-subcultures within the gay community: drag (male cross-dressing), professionals, bathhouses, Western style, the bar scene, and so on.

As people identify themselves as gay, they enter ever deepening levels of personal change. Everything in their lives, built around their new identity, constantly reinforces the strength of the bonds holding them in that false belief. To stay gay requires a huge emotional investment; to choose to exit a gay lifestyle may result in feelings of total loss of being: *This is my identity! If I give it up, what's left of me?*

So Who Is to Blame?

Maybe you are thinking, *Since many people struggling with homosexual sins were once victims, I shouldn't hold them accountable for their actions now. Perhaps it isn't entirely their fault, so God will overlook their homosexual problem.*

The Book of John presents an example of this type of thinking. In John 9, Jesus was confronted with a man, blind from birth. His disciples asked, "Whose sin caused it? His or his parents?" The Lord's answer was astonishing—"Neither hath this man sinned, nor his parents: but that the works of God should be made manifest in him" (John 9:3).

Jesus did not say that neither this man nor his parents were sinners; He said this case of blindness was not necessarily the result of either the man's or his parent's sin. But . . . the man was still blind! That was the situation the Lord wanted to remedy.

Now, physical blindness is not sin; homosexual "acting out" is. This is the point: Even if a person were predisposed to homosexuality due to the family situation or childhood trauma, that would *not* excuse homosexual actions.

You see, once the man was healed of the physical barrier of his blindness, he did not use it as an excuse to walk in spiritual darkness. When Jesus sought the man after he had been expelled from the temple for his forthright testimony, he willingly received Jesus as his Lord.

Likewise, an inclination to homosexuality would not be an excuse to walk in sin, once God has "opened our eyes." Rather, like any other sinful tendency where we recognize our weakness, it would be a cause to submit more areas of our character to the Holy Spirit's control.

God's dominion over the physical is limitless. He can easily heal physical needs. But He Himself limited His dominion over our will so we may have the opportunity to chose rightly. He will give us the ability to see, but He will not force us to walk in the light. That we must choose for ourselves.

This reasoning also applies to men and women who use their past pain as an excuse to continue in homosexual sin today. Few would deny that the experience of an emotionally broken child may cause such devastation as to promote a homosexual orientation. God is prepared to heal and bring release to the man or woman willing to walk in obedience. But once we are healed, our opened eyes are able to discern the right way and we are expected to walk in it.

Repeatedly, I have heard men and women who overcame homosexuality say, "If it weren't for this problem in my life, I'd never have sought God. This was too big—I couldn't do anything about it on my own." Yes, our God is faithful. As we recognize our deficiencies and inabilities and turn them over to Him, He will lead and guide us in the way we should go.

PART TWO

Reaching Out

About Fig Trees: Local Church Responses to Homosexuals and Homosexuality

THE REEDY, WARBLEY VOICE SANG THE HYMN SLOWLY, "THIS IS MY storrrrrry. This is my soooooooong."

Peeking around the door of the kitchen, I spoke, "Hi, Gramma. I didn't know you were here." Then looking down at the fruit in the sink, I exclaimed, "Oh, figs! Can I have one?"

"*May* I have one."

"May I have one?"

"Of course, dear." She handed me a just-washed fig.

It was dark purple, almost black. I smelled it with relish. A glistening drop of juice from a small break in the skin sparkled. Biting into the flesh, I said, "Ummm, these are so good. Your tree is a good tree, isn't it, Gramma?"

"It's a very good tree," she agreed.

And it continued to be a good tree for many more years, although growing old as Gramma did. One day, when Gramma was eighty-eight years old, she announced, "I'm going to put in a new fig tree this year. The old one isn't producing well anymore."

And so, taking her cane, she went to the nursery and hobbled through the aisles of fruit trees until she found the right one. My brother, Morris, planted it, according to Gram's instructions, voiced from the garden swing. "No, a little closer to the path there," she called, waving the cane. "That's it! Now we need a good deep hole."

Jesus, Fig Trees, and Religious People

Jesus taught in Matthew 21 about another fig tree, and the story becomes relevant to how to reach out to those exiting homosexuality: "And when he [Jesus] saw a fig tree in the way, he came to it, and found nothing thereon, but leaves only, and said unto it, Let no fruit grow on thee henceforward for ever. And presently the fig tree withered away. And when the disciples saw it, they marvelled, saying, How soon is the fig tree withered away!" (Matt. 21:19–20)

Why did our Lord curse the poor tree? Mark recounts in chapter 11, verse 13, "for the time of figs was not yet." Surely Jesus knew that figs were not in season. Why was He so hard on this fig tree?

On the surface, it would seem Jesus was just in a bad mood and took His anger out on a tree. But because we know the Lord, we know that could not be. The secret lies in the context of the passage and in a knowledge of fig trees.

The Lord had just made His triumphant entry into Jerusalem. He went directly to the temple and drove out the money changers and those who were selling animals. Then He returned the following morning. On the way to the temple, He passed the fig tree. What was Jesus thinking? What was His purpose in withering this tree? What were His feelings about what happened the previous day in the temple?

Jesus was outraged, and rightly so! But he did not allow that rage to be expressed sinfully. The Lord's words were a proclamation and a denunciation of the state of the tree—which was painfully similar to the state of the temple at Jerusalem and the entire nation of Israel.

Those who grow figs know that once the leaves begin to appear, there should also be buds of the fruit. But no fruit was on this fig tree, only leaves. The tree, possibly through age or disease, had quit producing. Though it had the appearance of vitality, everything the fig tree received went merely to maintain its own life.

And what about the religion being practiced in Jerusalem? How angry Jesus was when He saw the way the House of God was used. It only had the superficial appearance of life—just the "leaves." Rather than a place of prayer and worship, it had become a place of dishonest commerce.

The priests no longer ministered as true servants of God. They encouraged attendance for the purpose of their own wealth and prestige rather than furtherance of God's kingdom. Sacrifice had become a ritual that did nothing to cleanse or change hearts; it produced no fruit in the lives of people. Instead, it was only a means to maintain the status of a now stagnant religious organization and its ungodly rulers.

The withered fig tree was a bitter and harsh picture of the true condition of God's people. Though the tree looked healthy, it was dying from the inside. Though the temple looked prosperous and vital, it was only engaged in business—it was doing nothing to change the lives of people. Neither tree was bearing fruit.

The Modern Parallel

The temple leaders in Jesus' day were angry when He confronted their misuse of position. Jesus pointed out their spiritual coldness and hardness of heart. His truth cut through the lies with which they had surrounded themselves—lies they hid behind in order to continue in their wrong teachings, lies that polluted and perverted true worship of God.

Today, many church leaders, like the leaders in Jesus' day, twist the truth of Scripture about sin and homosexuality and mercy for their own purposes. And though the twisting can go in a number of different directions, ultimately all fail the test of compassion without compromise.

How do our churches measure up? If we were fruit trees instead of local outposts of Christianity, might we be withered if the truth were spoken? Churches respond to homosexuals and homosexuality in a variety of ways.

The Permissive Church

The permissive church defends a relaxed policy toward gay people. They are not concerned with the sin involved in homosexuality, though they may not openly endorse it. Rather, this church redefines sin according to current popular thinking. It often adopts a no-see, no-tell attitude toward homosexuality *and* many other sins.

The pastor of one permissive church recently told John Smid, director of Love In Action, "I just don't see it as a problem. Who are they hurting after all? How can we really say this is wrong?"

John, fixing his steel-blue eyes on this man, asked, "Pastor, have you ever been in the lifestyle?"

"Well, no, I haven't," he replied.

"Then," said John, "you really don't know the depth of depravity and how incredibly destructive homosexuality is to a person, do you? I was in homosexuality for four years. Believe me, it is sin and it brings a person to death."

The job of churches is to bring men and women to life in Jesus Christ. But the permissive church does not have a strong message of that hope. When Christ is presented there, He is not God, but rather a more human friend who has, through extraordinary sacrifice, obtained in the minds of men a special place of quasi-deity. He is not God enough to obey nor man enough to disrespect. His teachings are only teachings.

This church will most likely have some of the best programs for people with AIDS, which is admirable. They may sponsor events, incorporating other segments of the community, whose only link is the human need they benefit.

Paradoxically, though this church offers help to men and women who want to continue in sexual sin, they provide no comfort for those who seek help in overcoming homosexuality.

In brief, the permissive church is heavy on compassion but woefully short on truth.

The Rebellious Church

Church of the Open Door recently was contrasted with a "gay" church in San Francisco. The spin the media report gave was that theirs was the "loving" church (because it accepted gay people as they are) and ours was "harsh" (because we believe homosexual behavior is sin, but we help people change). Though the media often praises such accepting churches, I would say they are rebellious churches.

The rebellious church will have openly gay members. These members may even be very demonstrative in public and at services. They may be politically active and use the church to promote their agenda.

Members and leaders of these churches use all the parts of the Bible that keep them comfortable, but explain away anything that conflicts with their opinions. The rebellious church differs from the permissive church in one aspect: While the permissive church tends to ignore the teachings of Scripture, the rebellious church openly defies the Word of God.

Ultimately, then, this church rewrites the Bible to fit the beliefs of the congregation. In their view, people are more important than God; therefore, God could not have meant the things written in His Word. Often they will justify their position with statements such as, "God did not write the Bible; men wrote the Bible" and "Jesus never said anything about homosexuality being wrong."

The rebellious church does not want truth. It wants autonomy—self-defined authority—instead. And, for a time at least, its members have that authority. They live according to their own law, shaking their fists at both God and anyone else who opposes them. But then they die and enter eternity.

The rebellious church often has effective programs to care for people with AIDS and related illnesses. They will make an effort to reach out in the community to many who are infected with HIV, but the message of comfort they share will only be temporal comfort.

The Judgmental Church

In sharp contrast to the permissive and rebellious churches, which err on the side of compassion without truth, is the judgmental church, which errs on the side of truth without compassion.

Mary had been involved in lesbianism for ten years. Finally, God reached her, showing a better way and offering love and forgiveness through Jesus. After ending her relationship, she became a member in a church in North Carolina. Here she attended faithfully, involved herself in the life of the church, and tithed.

"One day," she confided to me, "I went to the pastor and told him I was still struggling with my emotions. Up to that point, I hadn't told him about my past. But I was so lonely. Someone had to know what I was going through! All I needed was some support, to know I was on the right track, and hear someone say they cared."

"Did he encourage you?" I asked. "Did he tell you how well you had done in coming so far?"

Mary shook her head. "No. He wanted to focus on what would stop me from struggling with the sin, but he had no plan for how I could be accepted and loved as I was. I tried to get him to understand that the sin was past. I needed help with my feelings."

"What do you mean? What sort of problems were you having?"

"Oh, I don't know," she sputtered bitterly. "I felt uncomfortable around other women, as if they knew all about how to be a woman and I didn't. And men, too. I knew how to relate to men as a lesbian, but not as a woman."

"Was there anything else? Did your pastor have any reason to question whether you were really done with the sin? Mary, had you completely left your lifestyle behind?"

"Yeah. But I was also honest about everything. I knew there might be years of having to confront sinful thoughts and feelings.

I also knew I needed the help of others to keep from falling back into lesbianism. When I asked for it, there wasn't any help there."

"His attitude must have been pretty discouraging. I can understand his approach, but it must have seemed as if he didn't trust you. Did you talk to others in church about your struggles?"

"I tried. It's not exactly something that comes up in everyday conversation! And you learn how to hide it so well. My best friend in high school never even knew. But when you talk to a church leader who responds, 'Don't tell me about the hurts. Let's just fix them,' you become pretty shy about sharing very openly with anyone else."

"What did you do?"

"I left the church. I just stopped going."

"What did they do when you quit? Did they try to make it right?"

Her face turned into an even more pained expression. "I *never* heard from them. I was still living in the same place, but no one ever contacted me. One family in the church still sends me Christmas cards, but they've never asked why I was still in the town but out of their church."

In my thinking, Mary had gone to a judgmental church. This church probably constitutes the largest group of theologically conservative Christian churches. Though standing for truth, judgmental churches give the law so forcefully that their members forget to mix in Christlike love that exhibits itself in compassion, patience, and willingness to help personally those who deeply desire transformation in their sexuality.

Mary's story sounds inconceivable. She attends a church, wants to clear up past sin in her life, and move forward as a vital part of the Body of Christ. That would seem to be the desire of every true member of Christ's family. Why did no one question her leaving? Why did no one reach out?

The silence from this church only reinforced Mary's alienation and loneliness when she was at a most vulnerable time. She needed the love of Jesus to be expressed by His people. Instead, whether through laziness, callousness, or just plain disobedience to the

Word, God's servants failed. This woman with a need just slipped through the cracks.

As her story illustrates, the judgmental church has sidestepped the entire message of the gospel. They have somehow forgotten that although people are hopelessly mired in sin and fail to keep God's Law, God's ever-present love and compassion have made a path for forgiveness through the death of His Son, Jesus Christ.

For this reason, people justifiably call the judgmental church hypocritical. Judgmental Christians only rescue the perishing if they can ensure their life preservers will come back clean and in good repair. It is not enough that this church knows God's truth, if they do not also display God's compassion and mercy.

Sadly, the gay community studies our failures. Often, lesbians and gays befriend abandoned overcomers at exactly this critical juncture and draw them right back into the world they have been trying to escape. What special tool or profound technique do they use? They simply reach out with love and acceptance. Of course, it is the counterfeit, but, being the sole offer, it is received, and many are thereby ensnared again.

The Uncommitted Church

The uncommitted church neither helps gays and lesbians out of their sin nor teaches a message that would convict them of sin. It says, "We don't know, so we can't get involved." It does not offer programs for people suffering from the roots and effects of the gay lifestyle (AIDS, depression, broken families, drug abuse, suicide, alcoholism, etc.).

Men and women in this church have a false sense of security. They fail to realize they have neither truth nor compassion. The leaders are misleading by default; that is, they fail to offer the clear guidance and direction the Lord expects from leaders for His church. Thus, the uncommitted church is in a most dangerous position. God is going to spit it out because its members are lukewarm (see Rev. 3:16).

The Ignorant Church

There is no excuse for ignorance on this topic! God has given clear instructions. The ignorant church simply does not know the truth of God. They may believe that homosexual involvement is wrong and that people who want out should be able to be helped. They just do not know how to help.

Ignorant Christians can only detract from the kingdom of God. Members of this type of church need to search God's Word and pray until the Lord shows them His truth and His will. God has great blessing if they will only listen and learn. Then instead of saying, "We want to help but we don't know how," they might actually become effective in ministry.

The Healing Church

Tim Rymel is Director of Outreach for Love In Action. Recently, he told me about what his pastor did right in handling his situation. Since Tim could not reconcile his Christianity with his homosexual desires, something had to give—and it did not appear to be his struggle against homosexuality.

During his time in church ministry, Tim led the singles group, taught Sunday school, led worship, directed the choir, and served in numerous areas of church leadership. But after two and a half years of ministry, he told his pastor he was resigning. He was tired of fighting the feelings and had finally decided to live his life as a homosexual.

"Pastor Jim," Tim said, "if Terry were a woman, we'd already be married. He makes me feel good about myself! He's brought up feelings in me that nobody else has. I don't know how the Bible fits into all of this, but I'm tired of living in this turmoil!"

His pastor sat quietly, listening to Tim's feeble excuses and rationalizations. "Watching my pastor's reaction had a profound effect," Tim said. "He listened intently. He acted as though he understood how I felt about Terry. He never appeared as though he were disgusted by what I was sharing.

"And then he responded with the words of a friend: 'Tim, I could quote all the Scriptures about homosexuality and tell you that it's wrong, but you already know that. I want you to know that *I* love you. I'm concerned about you. You've always had a special place in my heart, and I want you to know that I'm here for you whenever you need me.'"

Tim could almost feel the links of the chain that held him in bondage to homosexuality begin to break. "This man—my spiritual authority, my boss—showed me the kind of unconditional love that only Christ could give. And he did so in spite of my deepest, darkest secret. I told him I didn't know if I would be attending church there anymore. Jim simply smiled and said, 'Well, you're welcome here anytime.'"

It was not long before Tim broke off his gay relationship. Pastor Jim held true to his commitment. "In the months that followed, Jim made himself available to me for counseling and accountability. We remain friends to this day—four years after my coming out of homosexuality. Now he's my most faithful supporter in my outreach ministry to the gay community."[1]

Tim was fortunate. His pastor set the pace for a healing church. Such a church hears from God and obeys. Its members believe in the infallibility and authority of Scripture. Homosexual acting out is sin, and this church knows it. But they also know that for homosexual involvement—as for any sin—there is a complete and sure cure in the blood of Jesus Christ. And so this church balances biblical truth about homosexuality with the compassion of God for homosexual people as revealed through both His Word and His Son.

But the healing church goes beyond truth and into action. Its leaders commit to using their gifts to assist men and women overcoming homosexuality, just as they use their gifts to help anyone else with life-dominating sins. And other church members act on their willingness to serve as encouragers, accountability partners, and role models for overcomers.

The healing church allows God to do His work in the believer's life. It carries the message and offer of hope and support but does not try to drag people into wholeness. It may also have a formal program that reaches out to people suffering from the consequences of their sin.

In addition, this church will have a redemptive policy toward people who are HIV-positive or have AIDS. (By "redemptive" I mean it accepts people with HIV disease and seeks to help them resolve any underlying personal issues that may have led to their contracting this disease—drug abuse, sexual addiction, homosexuality, etc.)

An important aspect of the healing church will be the presence of church discipline. If and when people exhibit a true lack of desire to repent (that is, to turn away from the sins they contend with), this church will have leadership able to discipline them. This may take many forms, usually beginning with verbal correction and counseling. In extreme cases, it may lead to expulsion from the church and possible "disfellowshipping."

Ultimately, the healing church works because its leaders and members are committed to reaching out as individuals with mercy, grace, support, and the sometimes-hard-to-hear truth.

How About Your Church?

"Why don't you go to church now, Gramma?" I asked one Sunday.

"I don't feel that it's the same as it was," she said sadly. "The people are all different and the way they worship is different. I feel like a stranger there."

Gramma's church, like her fig tree, had grown old and was becoming barren. Should she have found another one? Replanted herself in a younger, more vital body of believers?

How about your church? Which type most closely fits the church body you call home? If you are not satisfied with the stands your church takes on issues of compassion without compromise, remember that revival can happen. Wrong teaching and doctrine can be righted. Sin can be disclosed, repented of, and forgiven. Hearts can be softened and turned again to the Lord and His plan for the future. Christians can learn to show mercy instead of judgment. But the people of God have to want it.

There is hope! Our God, the God of Resurrection Life, can restore the life that has gone. He can make dry and brittle branches once again supple and yielding, ready to bear fruit. And is that not our aim? To bring forth fruit and build the kingdom of God by His grace?

Building a Bridge: Our Individual Attitudes toward Overcomers

MIKE CAME INTO THE LIVING ROOM WHERE I WAS CAREFULLY storing away the last of the Christmas ornaments into huge boxes. "I heard that Kevin died," he said.

"Did he? That's a shame." But I really did not feel it was.

My mind flew back to another day when Mike and I sat talking. "But, Mike," I said, "Kevin must know that leaving the church this way is hurtful to the ministry. Has anyone talked with him?"

"He says we've talked enough."

"I thought he was doing so well spiritually. What happened anyway?"

"When his AIDS became full-blown, I think he just got scared. Maybe he thought God really wouldn't help him get through it. Whatever the reason, he's going in a different direction now."

"How do you keep from being angry with him, Mike?"

"Sometimes not very well. When I do, it's because I take it to God."

Kevin had offended many—particularly the leaders—before leaving our church. I felt betrayed then, and was still angry about it now.

How can I love You and have such a heart of stone, Lord?

Because you don't understand my forgiveness, Mona.

I want to. I want to feel grief for my brother. Lord, we loved Kevin and prayed for him through all his complications with AIDS. Why was he so awful to us? I get so tired of feeling used.

Mona?

Yes, Lord?

You haven't been used up yet.

I know, Lord. You shed Your blood for me.

Does it cleanse you?
Do you believe it cleanses you from all your sin?

Yes, Lord. I know it does. I know I'm forgiven.

Will it work for anyone? Everyone?

If they call upon You, Lord. It works for everyone.

Then why doesn't it work for Kevin?

What do you mean, Lord? It works for him too. He's forgiven.

Not by you. You claim My shed blood for *your* forgiveness
but you refuse to claim it for *Kevin's.*
If you can't believe it for him, you negate it for yourself as well.

Oh. I'm sorry, Lord. Can You do anything with me?

Well, you need to learn about My forgiveness.

How do I get over feeling used, Lord?

Why get over it?

Huh?

When you pray, don't you say to Me, "Use me?"
You are being used!
Don't mistake who is using you, though.
As *My* servant you are fulfilling *My* purposes.
I want you to trust Me for the wrong things this brother did.
They are My problem. You extend forgiveness.

But, Lord, he's already dead! How can I forgive him now? And what good would it do anyway? It won't make any difference to him.

It will make a difference to you, though.

The High Cost of Unforgiveness

I did stop and ask God's forgiveness for my hardened heart against my brother. God was good to remind me that when I refuse to extend forgiveness, my forgiveness from heaven is withheld. And I need His forgiveness—so I can't afford to withhold mine! As the Word reminds me: "And when ye stand praying, forgive, if ye have ought against any: that your Father also which is in heaven may forgive your trespasses. But if ye do not forgive, neither will your Father which is in heaven forgive your trespasses" (Mark 11:25–26).

Of course when someone sins against us, they should set it right. But what does it cost *us* if they do not? Have you ever thought about how wealthy you are? In His abundant love for us, God gave the most valuable gift He had to bestow. Everyone longs for eternal life. It is precious. We who have been graciously extended all our Heavenly Father's riches must surely be able to share with those who are impoverished.

Besides, God is the One who has been offended; nothing is taken away from me by someone else's sin. David said in Psalm 51: "Against thee, thee only, have I sinned, and done this evil in thy sight: that thou mightest be justified when thou speakest, and be clear when thou judgest" (v. 4).

This familiar verse reminds us that when we sin, it is accounted as an act of transgression against the laws of God and therefore against God Himself. Kevin was unkind to us as we tried to minister to him. He was sinning; but, though we were offended, he was sinning against God. And now I was sinning against God as well.

I remembered a conversation with my grandmother while washing her hair at the kitchen sink one lazy spring morning. On the patio outside, huge bumblebees made their rounds among the flowerpots as a hummingbird dipped in and out of the lathehouse, home of Gram's most exotic plants.

Looking away from the peaceful scene, I frowned as I soaped and rinsed. "I think Daddy's cancer is getting worse again, Gramma," I said. "He's lost more weight."

"Well, that will be very hard for him. He's not a man to endure weakness, especially his own," she replied offhandedly. Gramma was a Baptist raised in the south; Daddy was Jewish. They had never gotten along and never made a secret of it.

"Well," I tried again. "We need to pray for him."

"What for?" she asked.

"Why, of course, that he'll get saved."

"Saved? Him? He and I have never liked each other. Why should I pray to spend eternity in heaven with him?"

Incredibly shocked, I preached, "Gramma, we have to pray for him! You know God loves him, too. We've been put in his life to help him come to a saving knowledge of Christ. Our job is to forgive him and pray for him."

"He'll have to come without my prayers," she stated flatly. "I don't think he'd want to be there with me any more than I want him to be."

God answered my prayers for Daddy. I trust he and Gramma are getting along fine with Kevin there. Here, we are still trying to win over others like those three. Many ask for the path home to God. The Lord Jesus provided easy access to the Father through the cross. But how can we get them across the chasm leading to His kingdom and His people?

The Need on Both Sides

In the rolling hills of southern Sonoma County is a factory which produces fine cheeses from the milk of local dairies.

Earlier dairy farmers of this same part of California faced a dilemma in the 1920s. Milk was in great demand in San Francisco. But to sell to the large processing plants in the city, the dairy farmers of Marin, Sonoma, and other northern counties had to ferry their goods across the bay from one of several ports. The Steamer Gold ferry trip from the mouth of Sonoma County's Petaluma River took four hours. Since the boats did not have refrigerators, they placed milk at the prow so the cool air and spray would keep it fresh.

The passage from Sausalito in southern Marin County was faster, but still incredibly slow as a regular delivery route. While enduring the trip across the bay, more than one dairy farmer must have looked up at the cliffs of the Golden Gateway and wondered, *Why can't a bridge be built from Marin over to San Francisco?*

Likewise, on the San Francisco side there was a strong desire for a bridge. The people of the city wanted easy access to country living in the northern counties. Even today the original roads of Marin are still adorned with huge summer palaces of the San Francisco wealthy and influential from those earlier days.

As beautiful as the area was, even wealth and influence could not endear San Franciscans to the traffic along the Redwood Highway. Families might spend hours waiting for the ferry back home to the city on a busy Sunday afternoon.

Between citizens of Marin County and their counterparts in San Francisco yawned the wide, treacherous Golden Gate. Here the Sacramento River flowed out through Raccoon Strait and met the powerful longshore currents of the Pacific Ocean—creating unpredictable, swirling waters. Many engineers did not believe it possible to bridge the gap. In addition to the strong yet uncertain currents, the water was deep. The strength of the foundation rock on both sides was still undetermined. And never had a single span been built anywhere in the world to bridge so wide a distance.

We all know that today a bridge spans the Golden Gateway. But how did country farmers and city cosmopolitans finally get their bridge?

The Vision and the Sacrifices

The visionary responsible for the effort to build the Golden Gate Bridge was Joseph Strauss. Though his credentials as a builder were not the most prestigious, his vision was unerring. And he saw his dream built!

Strauss believed in the project when others said it could not be done. He staked everything on it—reputation, fortune, and future—in a campaign that lasted from 1919 to 1937. Little more than a year after completing the bridge, this engineer who had worked tirelessly to see it built was dead of heart failure. Joseph Strauss literally poured himself out as an offering for the vision in which he believed. His legacy and monument remains today.

But there will come a day when the foundation rock upon which it is built will no longer exist, and the Golden Gate Bridge will be gone with the rest of this world. When that day comes, the Christian women and men who have struggled to leave behind lesbianism and homosexuality will stand before God, their Salvation, and rejoice. Are we prepared to do whatever service God requires of us now to be able to rejoice with them then? That, and nothing less, is what God calls us to.

The Chasm Between

The obstacle before the people of God today is immense. On one side is the Christian church. On the other, those men and women who want to leave behind their homosexual lifestyles and the bondage that represents. Between these two lies a great chasm, swirling with fear and judgment, foaming with bitterness. Neither side has easy access to the other. Can a bridge be built between them?

The word from the media is that gays and lesbians are satisfied with their chosen lifestyles. Leaders of Love In Action know otherwise.

John Smid shared his frustration on this point, "One of the hardest things I face in ministry is turning away men and women who want to change and could be helped."

"Do you have to turn them away?" I asked.

He nodded bleakly. "We don't have room for them here. And in many parts of the country, there just is no organization to help these people."

And local churches are not always a helpful option because many brothers and sisters struggling with homosexuality are afraid to reveal themselves to people at church. So damaged have their relationships with the Christian community become that their level of trust is almost non-existent. One young man told me, "I just kept going to my church at the same time I was living the gay lifestyle. I couldn't tell anyone, not even the pastors. In the first place, the church was too large for me to have a personal relationship with my pastors. But there weren't even small group leaders I could talk to. I wanted help, but there was none. So I just kept it to myself."

Disgust over homosexuals' activities, fear of AIDS, and perhaps our own sexual insecurities fuel prejudice from the church side. In the face of militant gays or tragic deaths from AIDS, even the tenderhearted become hardened to the needs of these groups. And many in the church are not tenderhearted, but, like my grandmother and me, feel the right to give or withhold God's forgiveness according to whim.

How did the builders of the Golden Gate Bridge do it? What principles can we apply from their endeavors to help us in spanning our spiritual chasm?

A Sure Foundation

They began with a sure foundation. The bridge engineers took great pains to determine the exact composition of the foundation rocks on both sides of the Golden Gate. There were differing reports, questions as to whether the rock was solid enough to build upon. Not until they were sure the right support was there would planners even consider the project.

We need to be just as cautious in what we build upon. Our foundation must always be the Lord and the unerring surety of His Word. Without this to undergird our plans, we can never build the bridge. What does God say? Would He want us to reach out? Should we attempt a bridge between us?

Christ once asked: "What man of you, having an hundred sheep, if he lose one of them, doth not leave the ninety and nine in the wilderness, and go after that which is lost, until he find it?" (Luke 15:4).

Luke says Jesus asked this question in response to the murmuring of the Pharisees and scribes when they saw Jesus receiving publicans and sinners. The Lord knew sheep were a treasure to that community's men. He continued the lost sheep account, showing what He valued: "And when he hath found it, he layeth it on his shoulders, rejoicing. And when he cometh home he calleth together his friends and neighbours, saying unto them, Rejoice with me; for I have found my sheep which was lost. I say unto you, that likewise joy shall be in heaven over one sinner that repenteth, more than over ninety and nine just persons, which need no repentance" (Luke 15:6–7).

A good foundation exists for reaching out to those who want to walk away from *any* sin. They are the treasure that God seeks in this world.

Building Upward

The two towers of the Golden Gate Bridge each had to be built on the foundation that was laid. But neither extends itself across to the tower on the other shore. They are separated. Jesus pointed out in Luke 15 that sinners are not separated from God after they repent, but often they remain separated from other family members: "And he said, A certain man had two sons: And the younger of them said to his father, Father, give me the portion of goods that falleth to me. And he divided unto them his living. And not many days after the younger son gathered all together, and took his journey into a far country, and there wasted his substance with riotous living. And when he had spent all, there arose a mighty famine in that land; and he began to be in want" (Luke 15:11–14).

This young man fell into deep sin. His story tells of his slide into depravity and the wretched poverty that resulted. Many who have fallen into the sins associated with homosexuality find themselves in a similar situation. Although raised in the household of faith, many foolishly took the blessings of their Heavenly Father and squandered their lives in drunkenness and fleshly pleasures. Others were rescued in the midst of their sin by a God they did not know. In either case, having come to themselves, they wanted desperately to return from the far country of homosexuality or lesbianism.

As they turned to God, they began to walk into wholeness in Him. In such cases, there was and is no bridge between them and the Lord, for there is no gap between the repentant heart and God. But to work that out with the others of the father's household is sometimes a different story. Like the prodigal's brother, church people are not always very forgiving: "Now his elder son was in the field: and as he came and drew nigh to the house, he heard music and dancing. And he called one of the servants, and asked what these things meant. And he said unto him, Thy brother is come; and thy father hath killed the fatted calf, because he hath received him safe and sound. And he was angry, and would not go in" (Luke 15:25–28a).

The prodigal son had to endure the long journey back from the far country to which he had wandered. He had come to a state of true repentance and brokenness. Humbly, he chose to go back. In that attitude of humility he found forgiveness in the arms of his father. The father had watched for his son coming from afar and went to him.

But what of the brother who hardened his heart? He did not join the joyous festivities when his erring brother returned. Instead, he questioned his father's judgment. The prodigal was restored to his father's household, even though his unforgiving brother refused to take part in his welcome: "Therefore came his father out, and entreated him. . . . And he said unto him, Son, thou art ever with me, and all that I have is thine. It was meet that we should make merry, and be glad: for this thy brother was dead, and is alive again; and was lost, and is found" (Luke 15:28b, 31–32).

The elder brother had nothing to lose by embracing his younger sibling at his return. Rather, as the father pointed out, he retained all. And most importantly, he now gained his brother, who was as dead.

Isn't that what we want—to see those who are lost become found? To see the dead brought into life eternal? Or are we like the older brother, questioning God's judgment and perhaps even the salvation of some who have been redeemed? Have we built a tall tower up toward God from which we can look across the unbridged expanse and feel superior? Are we fearful that God's kingdom will suffer from their salvation? Do we worry about our being spiritually "contaminated"?

Did these hypothetical brothers ever become joined? The Scriptures do not reveal the outcome. I like to think they were reconciled to each other, based on their relationship with a wise and loving father. I know that we, whether in the church or in the "ex-gay" movement, can only be reconciled through our Heavenly Father. Do we want to see the gap bridged between the church and gays and lesbians who yearn for our help in changing their identity and orientation?

Building from Both Sides

What would it be like if there were no bridge?

That, unfortunately, is the case for many men and women struggling with homosexuality and trying to find acceptance and understanding in the church. They find no bridge to cover the gap between the past they want to leave behind and the love and understanding they desire from the people of God.

Will the church today meet these overcomers with the welcome God ordains His servants have for all repentant sinners? For we must never forget that we are called as servants. We build expectantly toward our Father in heaven, and when our relationship with Him is solid, we are ready to reach out to the rest of His creation.

Like the builders of the Golden Gate Bridge, we anchor into our foundation and build upon it a tower reaching upward. When the towers were high enough and strong enough, there was support to build toward the other side. They spanned the geographic gap, and we need to span the spiritual gap.

What side do you come from? Are you a member of a church that needs to minister to lesbians and gays? Build a tower to God and then a bridge to people in need. Are you a gay or lesbian in need of guidance and help as you labor to leave that lifestyle behind? Build a tower to God and then construct a span from your side as well, forgiving the church of past negligence.

We must build in faith toward each other. Faith believes the tower will hold as we construct our part of the span. Faith believes someone else will build toward us. Faith trusts we will meet somewhere in the middle, by God's grace, like the clasped hands of two brothers reunited.

The actual Golden Gate Bridge project took four years and cost 18 million dollars. Eleven men lost their lives. Today the trip from my home in San Rafael to my sister's home in San Francisco takes about thirty minutes. I seldom think much about the bridge; I just drive over it and back again. The men and women who made the many investments necessary to build it, however, laid the road for my future access.

That is what the whole church today can do if we make the right choices. Will we ignore, or worse, turn away this group? Or will we build a bridge to them, a road which—though narrow—supplies a pathway back into the Father's household? Never forget, they are already in His arms. It remains for us to make them welcome in His earthly home.

It is good to know our responsibilities. But if we do not receive any "how-to's," we will build a bridge without a blueprint. The next chapter looks at some of the ways healing of the homosexual can take place and how we can take part in this ministry. And we will look at several lives that were changed when someone reached out to welcome a brother or sister home.

CHAPTER SEVEN

No Balm in Gilead: Why and How to Help Overcomers

"I'M WONDERING IF YOU'D BE WILLING TO SPEND SOME TIME WITH me?" the voice on the phone asked tentatively.

Lord, how am I going to find time for someone else?
You have enough time for Kitty.
I'm already swamped! Maybe someone else could meet with her.
She's asking you.

Still I hesitated . . . too long. She spoke up again.

"Oh, well, I mean, I know you're really busy and I didn't mean you had to spend a lot of time. Just maybe you could call me when you have some extra space on your calendar and we could get together and talk."

Kitty was a sensitive, talented woman who gave freely of her time and energy to our church and the Love In Action program. We were only acquaintances. I knew she had been a lesbian, but now she had turned her life over to the Lord. Beyond that, this woman was a mystery to me.

I'm sorry, Lord. Help me share your love for Kitty. Put her at ease.

"Kitty, I'd love to get together with you," I said and meant it. "What's good? How about taking a walk?"

"Great! I love to walk! How about Saturday morning?" The excitement in her voice was contagious.

"I'll look forward to it," I said. "Let's say, 9:00 A.M."

That phone call began a precious friendship. Kitty shared her full testimony, helping me understand the lesbian lifestyle from the other side. She also honored me with questions about the Lord, how to go on in a church such as ours, and my insights into being a woman in today's world. Kitty honestly told me her feelings about men, her fears and frustrations, and areas where she felt weak and strong. "I just want your opinion," she would begin, and then we would talk and talk. If I would say, "I think that passage is in Jeremiah," she would pour over the entire book before our next meeting.

God blessed me abundantly because I decided to set aside some time for someone who asked. I have thanked Him again and again because I know that without the prompting of His Spirit, I would likely have been selfish enough to ignore Kitty's request. And God gave great blessings to Kitty, because she became an obedient disciple of His and a faithful woman.

Often I find myself asking if I have a proper response to the heartfelt need of those caught up in a gay lifestyle. Do I have compassion on their loneliness and answers that really work? Do you? What about complete healing? Do we really believe it is possible for *any* sin? Must we admit that Christianity does not always work? Do we know if there is balm in Gilead?

Is There Balm in Gilead?

The Lord asked just this question of the nation of Israel through the mouth of the prophet Jeremiah. Israel suffered greatly because of their sin. They would soon suffer more.

Why? Why were they so sin-sick, when the Lord God of all the universe had set His special affection upon them and blessed them beyond any other nation? The prophets repeatedly stated that Israel was disobedient—unfaithful to God. Looking to the gods of nations around her, she sinned repeatedly. Her people were polluted with idolatry. And so, though the need was very great, Israel could not find healing.

The irony of the question Jeremiah asked was this: The healing balm of Gilead, well-known throughout the world in that day for its medicinal properties, came from within their own land and was compounded by those skilled in its use. (No one is exactly sure how the balm of Gilead was made or even what trees or other plants its components came from. Suffice it to say that it worked, and it became a byword for healing.)

This prophet sought to show his compatriots that God could heal all their wounds and restore their nation, if they would just return to Him and allow the application of the salve He prepared. To Jeremiah's deep sorrow, they would not.

And what of us? Jesus has graciously dispersed throughout the Body of Christ the hope for healing in this day. But are we dispensing it? Do we apply the salve when someone comes, wounded and sick? Or do we simply sigh over the sadness of their past sin and offer suggestions for further cleansing to those who have already been washed in the flood of our Lord's forgiveness and acceptance?

So how, practically speaking, can we act in ways that will soothe the wounds of these precious saints and help them on the road to living out God's design?

Count *Their* Cost

Sometimes people feel uncomfortable about getting close to men and women overcoming homosexuality. Maybe they have never known anyone gay or formerly gay and are fearful. They wonder, *What are they thinking when they look my way? Will they try to seduce me?* Maybe they do know someone and have been disgusted or hurt.

But put yourself in the place of gays and lesbians for a moment. Consider that a homosexual person is leaving behind so much more than just a sexual sin. Calling gay a lifestyle is completely correct. To exit it requires a complete lifechange. To become "ex-gay," a man or woman often has to walk away from a lover, a support network of friendships, a job, a home, and an entire way of doing things.

On top of everything else, a person who chooses to deal with his or her homosexuality must endeavor to change personality traits he or she has spent years establishing. The feelings of masculinity or femininity are often wrong. Responses to others of the same sex, as well as the opposite sex, may be contrary to the truth. Could you make such radical personal and lifestyle alterations alone?

Go Two by Two

Forsaking any sin has inherent difficulties. We need prayer support and accountability that comes from close relationships with caring brothers and sisters. Jesus Himself sent out His disciples in pairs, knowing that they would support one another. What Kitty needed more than anything else was someone to walk with her as a friend.

The changes Kitty made in her life were right in God's sight, but they felt wrong in her experience. Someone who knew the truth—that Kitty's choices *were* right—gave her support. Kitty longed for encouragement to continue through the awkwardness and loneliness of this period in her life.

So when someone asks for help, the first step is to offer your friendship. You befriend an overcomer the same way you befriend any other sinner. How do you get to know people? What makes them feel welcome? There is always a meeting ground in our common need for Jesus' love and forgiveness and in our communion together as recipients of His grace.

Unquestionably, gays and lesbians have walked in deception. We must teach and encourage them as they walk in truth. God's people have to shine the light on a pathway grown dim. In addition, people overcoming homosexuality need proper role models—to see the truth in action. You can be someone they can watch and learn from, someone who is both accessible and approachable. That is what Kitty was after and why she responded so well. She had a teachable spirit and faithfully applied what she observed in, and learned from, me.

Keep in mind overcomers generally are eager to learn, but inevitably make mistakes. If we provide good examples of right choices, however, we can minimize the damage.

Count *Your* Cost

Friendliness is important, but so is a willingness to persevere through unpleasant problems and conversations, so that your friend might find help and hope. For instance, people who have never been involved in homosexuality often find themselves shocked and disturbed by the plain speaking they encounter. On many levels, overcomers tend to be pretty open about their lives. At times I was shocked to hear frank discussion about past lovers, private feelings and desires, childhood molestation, or current temptations. These men and women often feel they are hanging on, at times just by a thread. Sometimes they cannot afford to observe all the niceties of proper social interaction, even if they know them. They sense themselves slipping away! How should we respond?

Our job is not to be shocked or reactionary, but to bring out a fresh supply of compassion and understanding to meet each new challenge. Remember Jesus' encounter with the ten lepers? Can you imagine how they must have appeared? The filth and human abomination that assailed our Lord as He looked upon these men is hard to picture. When they reached out decaying fingers for help, Jesus did not allow horror to turn Him away from their healing. Our Lord was unflappable in the face of these men He had created; His is the example of spiritual concern we should follow.

At first, the common frankness in sharing personal struggles may make you feel like withdrawing. But you may well find what many "straight" men and women in Church of the Open Door have discovered: The honesty and reality becomes both refreshing and a challenge. I continually see positive impact as all our members interact and learn from each other.

One final suggestion concerns adjustments in conversation. As you establish a deeper friendship with someone exiting homosexuality, encourage him or her to use clinical terms to describe sexuality issues—not street language or gay slang terminology. This is another way to help re-establish a respect for their bodies which God created. It also helps make a break with the gay community, because gay topics and lingo may have become a pervasive crutch for communicating.

Healthy Boundaries

Years ago, Tom, a former gay, attached himself to my husband, Mike. I use the word *attached* because it is pretty descriptive of what their relationship was like. Tom called daily, just wanting to share news of the day and find out how Mike's day had gone. He dropped by unannounced on a regular basis, often infringing on family time.

Gradually, Tom visited more and more and requested more time. Mike and I realized it was unfair to allow him to depend upon us rather than upon God. When Mike finally talked with him about their relationship, Tom was offended and hurt. Our friendship died off. He eventually left the church.

This taught us a tough but valuable lesson. When you invite someone to be honest with you, you must be straightforward in return. There is no room for pretense, even when your motives are good. To be effective for someone else's healing, a church must provide both accurate information and affirming relationships. Yet every friendship requires boundaries. Often we establish them subconsciously, without any intention. However, our relationships with overcomers must have clear guidelines. It is safer to err on the side of caution—and you may need to be the one to invoke that rule.

Do you feel smothered in the relationship? Say so! Emotional dependency is a fairly common problem, particularly with former lesbians. This type of confused, emotional entanglement leads to exclusive friendships, jealousy, speaking on behalf of the other person in the relationship, and generally losing track of the boundaries between two people. Many lesbians and some gay men

related to their old friends this way. Now they must develop ultimate dependency upon Jesus. Keep redirecting their love toward
Him, and help them come to a true sense of themselves—apart
from anyone else but God.

Helping with Externals

Another way to give honest information is in matters of personal
presentation. How does he or she come across? For instance, if a
woman wonders which lipstick color is best and you know it will
not matter if she continues to chew tobacco, honesty should com-
pel you to tell her the truth. Be nice about it but truthful. "Lipstick
won't make you look or feel more feminine with a plug of tobacco
in the corner of your mouth. Let's work on the chewing first." This
may seem preposterous, but it has been my experience!

Remember, the object is not to add more weight of law to
someone who is already struggling. Affectations do not disappear
overnight, but some obvious habits can. If that same woman is also
overweight, common sense should tell you to leave it alone. Help
her learn how to dress well with the body she has. As much as
possible, show her ways to express her femininity within the context of who she is today.

I saw this principle of taking change one step at a time perfectly
illustrated one day. Before becoming a Christian, Sy had been on
female hormones and lived for over two years as a woman in
preparation for a sex-change operation. Some of the effects on his
facial features and mannerisms had not left yet. Now, as a leader in
a ministry to people from homosexual backgrounds, he was on a
national talk show.

A man from the audience spoke up quite candidly, "You say you
have given up the gay lifestyle, but you still look and sound pretty
effeminate to me."

"You think so," retorted Sy. "Listen, Buster, this is light years
away from pink panty hose!"

In short, first things first. Pray and start helping with the key
changes first. Don't force them to take on too much at one time.

And continue being a vulnerable role model of godly masculinity or femininity.

Beyond Externals

Safe experimentation is a necessary and valid part of any healing. So another aspect of ministry involves providing overcomers with opportunities to try out what they learn about relating appropriately. This brings us back to the fences we use to keep us from overstepping our limits. Testing within confidence-building parameters can be very healthy.

One of the ways we've seen this happen is at events like square dances. Many men and women from Love In Action come to these with a lot of unease. It may be hard for them to hold a member of the opposite sex, even by the hand. But it can be a way to try out what they are learning in a protected environment, where guidelines are strictly delineated.

Our makeup classes do the same, as well. Most women learn about things like cosmetics while growing up. That may not be the case with lesbian women. How do they find out now without seeming very foolish? Often, the job of coming alongside is little more than presenting new ideas in a non-threatening way. We do not expect all the women to start wearing cosmetics, but we do want them to begin experimenting with some of the cultural trappings of femininity.

Similarly, a man who believed himself to be gay may have eschewed sports like baseball. Now someone should teach him—not because baseball is an important part of masculinity, but because he may gain confidence with his newfound knowledge and feel he fits in with the rest of the guys at church.

Taking Initiative

Another chance for growth is at our church's annual men's and women's retreats. For example, a man overcoming homosexual desires often finds sleeping near other men in a community bunkroom a big challenge. It must and should be a safe one. By taking the initiative, the other men can make it so. They ought to be aware of his special needs and yet not treat him differently. Healthy, brotherly hugs often bring great confidence when a man realizes for the first time, "I didn't experience any wrong desire when he hugged me!"

Bill was in a gay lifestyle many years before coming to Love In Action. The night he and his fellow program members were introduced was profound for him. "I'd never been hugged by a man in the right way, you know, without it being a sexual thing. My dad never would have hugged me. I don't blame him for my sin, but I grew up craving the love of a man. I got it all wrong in homosexuality. But at Love In Action Night, I got it right. For the first time a man hugged me and I felt real affirmation—as if someone was proud of me."

The Long Haul

One right response rarely causes permanent change in anyone's life. Thus, everyone must have reasonable expectations of the transformation process. I saw this recently while talking with a young man in his second year of Love In Action's live-in program. We met at church and I greeted him. "Hi, Phillip. How are you doing?"

The look in his eyes told me clearly, though all he said was, "Oh, I'm struggling a bit."

From experience, I know that "struggling" may mean anything from feeling blue, to serious doubting, to actually falling into sin. So I probed deeper. "What's going on?"

Sadness and frustration mingled in his voice, "I had no idea this second year would be so hard! Last year, when second-year guys were having trouble, I didn't understand it. Now I see. I'm having to deal with things again that I thought I'd finished. It's pretty discouraging."

Phillip was learning that the changes he had experienced, though real, were only a beginning. He needed to adjust his expectations, just as we who wrestle with other types of problems must. God has much more deep healing to do and *God is not hasty!* Rather, He is a careful, meticulous Master Craftsman in all the lifework He accomplishes.

It is like our back yard area for growing vegetables. When my children were little, we planted carrots and radishes, green beans and tomatoes. All three kids loved to plant the seeds and were thrilled when the shoots emerged. But between the excitement of a strong beginning and the fulfillment of a good crop lay weeks and even months of consistent care. Tiring days spent tending the plants in the sun seemed fruitless when a small, impatient hand pulled up an immature radish and a little voice moaned, "When will they be ready?"

Phillip needed growing time and more patience with his failures. Does that mean he could not expect a full restoration in his life? Absolutely not! He can and will, if he continues to pursue God's best—the same as for any of us. We can help by holding up realistic expectations for change, especially by talking about some stubborn habits and sin patterns in our own lives that have been slow to transform.

Jesus does not want us to make just a good start! He wants every child of His to experience life abundantly. It will not happen at one square dance, one "make-over" class, one year of friendship. But by God's grace, it will happen. And a friend and mentor who applies the healing balm of Gilead will literally make a world of difference for that one man or woman who deeply desires wholeness in his or her sexuality.

CHAPTER EIGHT

Planting for Success: Essential Ingredients for Transformation

WHAT MAKES ONE PERSON'S GARDEN FLOURISH WHILE A NEIGHbor's struggles? We say he has a green thumb. Is it really a special blessing or talent, or are there guidelines which can make anyone successful with plants? What does it take to plant something anyway? You need soil and seed. But what does it take to plant something *well*, so that it will grow successfully? Obviously, not just any soil and not just any seed.

Good Soil for Growth

The house was unnaturally quiet. Mike and the kids had gone on an errand, and I enjoyed a respite from the din of family life. *Ringgg!* The phone intruded.

"Hello."

"Mona? Is that you?" the voice asked.

"It's me," I replied. "Who's this?"

"Anne. Do you have a minute?"

(I often wonder why people ask if you have a minute when it is clear from the outset that *one* will never do.) But I said, "Of course, Anne. What's up?"

"Well, John and I have been dating for a while and he's invited me out on a 'special' date." She gasped. "I just know he's going to ask me to marry him! I'm so excited, but . . . I want to look my best. Do you think you could help me?"

"I'd love to help you. Can you come over now? We'll work on a knock-out look!"

"Great. That's perfect. Should I bring the makeup I've got?"

"Mm-hum. And be sure to bring everything you plan to wear, even jewelry." I hung up the phone and smiled.

I remember Michael's face when he came home from the office that afternoon. "It's happened!" he practically shouted. "John is going to ask Anne to marry him this weekend."

"That's terrific!" I laughed, hugging him.

Both John and Anne had come out of a gay lifestyle. Both were going on to a new level in their healing. It was frightening, exciting, and very fulfilling to watch. They were godly people who had worked hard and struggled through times of stumbling and doubting. Mike and I felt pride in their accomplishments in Christ, much as we might with our own children.

I first got to know Anne through a makeup class I taught for the women in the Love In Action live-in program. Cosmetics can be frightening for a woman who has always avoided anything feminine. Not all the women could handle the altered face looking back in the mirror. Some of them were not ready for change.

What makes the difference for healing? What was it that enabled Anne to receive the healing and change she desired while others could not? The main difference was the soil. Anne was very receptive to God's truth as revealed in His Word.

Sometimes, to our amazement, healing takes place all at once. But more often it is a seed planted and nurtured by first turning to God and then continuing in His truth. That does not mean we cannot work with those who are not yet receptive or that they cannot be healed, but they have to be ready to walk through a lot of brokenness.

Hard Ground

Where I live in California, we suffer with an underlying layer of clay that makes gardening a true challenge. Clay is interesting stuff. Though full of nutrients, clay particles are small. Its ultra-compact structure allows no room for water to penetrate. Although full of all good things plants need to grow, it supplies a poor medium for growth.

For plants to get to those nutrients, the clay first must be broken up, and then the friable or broken state maintained. That is why California farmers work rice hulls or other plant matter into the soil. Seeds dropped in "repaired" clay soil grow well, having room to push their roots down and receive the water and nutrients no longer locked in the clay mass.

Many persons' lives are a bit like clay soil. Though full of potential, they have become hard or compacted. They are not even able to receive the "seed" of God's Word. No matter how much we try to plant the truth—no matter how often we water—until the soil becomes broken and the right things added to it, nothing good will be planted and take root.

If people who become hard in life allow God to break them—uncovering the wounds that hardened them in the first place—we see great change. Their ongoing brokenness provides God access to work His living Word into them. Keeping the "soil" or substance of their lives open means a man or woman stays receptive to progressively more truth, taking them to deeper levels of healing.

An insightful biblical illustration of this principle is the cleansing of Naaman the Leper (2 Kings 5). He was a great commander of men and highly esteemed in Syria. Through a messenger, the prophet Elisha told him to dip himself in the Jordan River seven times. Naturally, Naaman was angry that the man of God did not even bother to come in person and pray over him. He started to leave in a rage.

What happened? His servants kindly entreated him, and Naaman humbly went and did as he was bid. How foolish this leader must have felt. How ridiculous he looked to those lacking understanding. And yet, Naaman was healed in the course of acting obediently. His pride could have robbed him of his healing, but he let God break up his haughtiness instead. This military man's desire to obtain healing transcended his feelings about what he had to do to obtain that healing.

To find healing, sometimes we must actively walk through situations that make us seem foolish. But our response of obedience helps break up clay soil that keeps us from receiving nutrients of love and forgiveness. Easy to say, hard to do. In fact, without the help of God, it is impossible.

Naaman was healed, but he had to dip himself seven times. He was not healed the first time, nor the second nor third. Rather, he had to continue obediently, fulfilling all that God required. And if the great leader had not listened to his servants—first the little Jewish maid and then those who went with him to Elisha—he would never have known how to be healed.

What about us? If we learn new ways of righteous responses, can we be assured of a good outcome? If we listen to God's servants around us and walk in obedience to His Word, will we be healed?

Do I Want God or Merely His Blessing?

Why would anyone want to stop committing the sin of toying with homosexual thoughts or acting upon them? Yes, God's Word clearly states these as sin, so God's servants should want to stop committing them. Many people are not happy in lesbianism and homosexuality, but many remain there.

What draws men and women out of darkness and continues to lead them on when the way is lonely and the road increasingly narrow? Do they merely want to be happy and forgiven? Or is it something else? Why are we really motivated to change our wrong ways and learn His right ways?

In chapter 4 we discussed differences between "gay" and "homosexual." Those who chose a gay identity and lifestyle often still strongly desire to please God. One church I learned of teaches its members that gay and lesbian "marriages" must be monogamous for God to bless them. That is, their lives in other respects must be "Christian"—no infidelity allowed.

I am convinced a true desire to live according to God's law keeps men and women in this church. Sadly, these people erroneously believe that if they satisfy God in everything else, they can continue in the one thing they do not want to give up. This is not devotion; it is bargaining. And to whatever extent you are unwilling to forsake something fleshly, to that same extent you cannot grow in Christ. Or, as Love In Action founder Frank Worthen says, "The height of your victory is equal to the depth of your surrender."

God calls upon us to sacrifice. Christ, our perfect example, died to redeem us, giving Himself. To the extent that we hold on to an unholy thing, we are unwilling to carry out our love in sacrifice to God. If we say we love Him and want to be devoted, how willing are we to die to self?

Dying to self is the wall many people hit. They not only retain a gay identity but also demonstrate a strongly self-oriented value system. Their homosexual lifestyle makes them unhappy, and they are convicted that it is wrong. That is why people come to a ministry like Love In Action. But often men and women falter after they stop the sexual involvement part of homosexuality. Why? Because they fail, at a heart level, to deal with the fact that homosexuality is the result of their underlying rebellion toward God. When they turn away from the acting out of their sin, they often become satisfied and are not interested in pleasing the Lord further.

Anne, on the contrary, had come out of the gay scene but had made a true commitment to a self-sacrificing value system. Her driving desire was to know God better and please Him. The deep change in her interior life resulted in a dramatic exterior transformation. The before and after pictures of her life are simply incredible! She went from an extremely "butchy" lesbian with severe lines and cropped hair to a feminine woman with soft lines and longer hair. You would *never* have guessed at her past.

Anne's success was predictable because she had decided God's Word is right—homosexual and lesbian involvement is wrong. Her initial motivation to change may have grown out of a need to bring healing into her own life, but as she walked in obedience, her continuing choices for change were the product of ever-deepening levels of devotion to God and His call to obedience. Others want healing, but it appears that is *all* they want—healing, yes, but the

Healer ... not necessarily. Thus, they cannot enter into wholeness or service.

Our Lord loves gardening, but He spends a lot of time preparing the soil in your life and mine. We can avoid this often painful and unpleasant process simply by saying no and walking away. Many people who have come a long way choose to do just that. What a shame! If they would just allow the Gardener to break up the clods of clay and add in whatever is needed to keep the soil broken, they would be ready for what God wants to plant.

Anne had given her life over to a system of theocracy, where God rules supreme—even over her desires. That empowered her to move on with Him, and now it is obvious her femininity is not role-playing but real. Scores of men and women have discovered Anne's "secret" for success: steadfast commitment to following God's Word and eschewing sin—and not just homosexual sin—even if their homosexual feelings never diminish. This principle has been borne out repeatedly through Love In Action's live-in programs and support groups, and through more than one hundred ministries worldwide in the Exodus International network.

Of course, I am not speaking of mere willpower here, but of a deep, heart commitment to follow Him in truth, regardless. That makes for good soil. But what of good seed?

Seeds: After Its Kind

Great-gramma Holder's farming family settled in the hills of North Carolina. Although my grandmother became a nurse, she always was a farmer in her heart. Wherever she lived, she would plant a garden; whenever she planted, the garden flourished. As Gramma aged, she kept gardening, though her efforts lessened and her gardens shrank. But it seemed no matter how small the plot she tilled, there were always green beans.

"These aren't just any beans, you know," she said one day with a knowing nod. "My mother's family has grown these same beans for generations. None better—they're crisp and sweet but the skin is tender, not thick like some you might taste." Here she wrinkled

her nose and nodded again for emphasis. "I took seeds from mother's garden years ago. And every year I could, I grew at least enough plants for more seed. They'll keep a long time in the fridge, so this year you be sure and get some when we pick them. Then you folks will have some for your garden, too."

That year was her last bean crop, for she was sick in the spring and died in May. I did get some of the wonderful beans from her garden so I could carry on with them. They do produce good green beans, smaller than others, but very tasty. They will not produce a long green bean, nor are they fat and juicy. Gramma's green beans are all that grow from her green bean seeds. If you want something else—different taste or size, for instance—you'll have to plant some other seed.

The Bible says, "And the earth brought forth grass, and every herb yielding seed after its kind, and the tree yielding fruit, whose seed was in itself, after its kind: and God saw that it was good" (Gen. 1:12). Each type of plant produces fruit and seed peculiar to that plant. If you want something else, you'll have to plant something else. As it is in the plant world, so it is in the lives of men and women. People grow spiritually and emotionally according to what has been planted in them.

Do you remember Sylvia's story from chapter 1? Failure to develop in her birth gender had been planted in her from childhood onward. Alienation from her mother brought a corresponding alienation from her mother's gender, and thus, her own. And yet, as a child, she naturally desired the emotional intimacy she should have experienced with her mother. She later transferred that unfulfilled emotional need onto other women as a sexual "need." This all served to block Sylvia from enjoying the femininity that was her birthright. She could not reap success. Failure was growing and bearing a bitter harvest in a lifestyle of lesbianism. How could Sylvia change what she reaped?

Uprooting and Reseeding

Everybody who gardens has known failure with some planting. I experience this constantly as I tend to have more enthusiasm

than knowledge, but my frequent gardening mistakes school me well. Once I realize that something is growing where it should not—where it will affect the future of the garden I want—I must uproot it and replant the area with the correct variety of vegetation.

Sylvia had already seen this principle of uprooting and reseeding at work in her life. Growing in her was a lack of identification with a feminine gender. She needed to continue these processes that began the day she came to Jesus, asked His forgiveness, and started the long uphill climb out of lesbianism. First, she uprooted that wrong plant by agreeing with God in whom He had created her to be—a woman.

Many people involved in homosexuality believe that somewhere along the way God made a mistake and created them with the wrong gender. That this is only perceptual does not make it seem any less real. And yet we all have areas of our lives where we wonder if God made a mistake. We all question whether we were created exactly as God wanted us. From super-models to superstars to super-athletes, no one is truly satisfied with themselves. Even we Christians must admit we are not satisfied with everything about ourselves. And if you were able to recreate yourself to be completely satisfied, you would then begin to *age!* Face it: Life is not meant to lead to perfection—quite the opposite.

But what happens when *everything* about your life is dissatisfying? That can be the perception when a person rejects his or her gender. Does personal dissatisfaction mean that life is truly bad? Of course not. One pastor's wife I know always responds to her children when they say, "But Mom, it's not fair!" by saying, "Life's not fair. It's a blessing."

God has a good plan for each life that, if lived out, will lead to life eternal and complete satisfaction. Sometimes those things which seem the least fair are the truest blessings in our lives if we allow God to use them for His purpose.

Implementing God's plan for me means first I must agree with it. That begins by accepting myself as God created me. In Sylvia's case that meant she first had to agree that God had not made a

mistake in creating her a woman. She had to uproot the lie of being made "wrong" and replant with the truth that God had indeed made her as He intended her to be. Then she had to undergo whatever God gave to fulfill His purpose in her life and bring her to the perfection He desires for all His children. Like Naaman obediently washing seven times, she had to allow God to rule supreme and seek to please Him.

If you had asked my grandmother what were the best seeds for green beans, she would have told you to plant her mother's seeds. They would produce the crop she wanted.

There is only one right seed to sow in the lives of men and women if you want to produce healthy men and women. That is the one that lay in a tomb three days and then rose from the dead. Sometimes in the process of following Christ we feel that we are dying. Paradoxically, that is the idea!

Gender Security: Making the Link

Back to Anne's story. When Anne got to my home, we tried different looks on her. We discussed her feelings and fears. Not for a minute did I reveal what I already knew about John's purpose in their special date.

"He has such definite ideas about what he likes," she moaned. "What if I'm not it?"

"Just go planning on a good time. Don't worry about what might happen."

"I've never been so scared in my life! What if he asks me to marry him?"

"You're asking *me*? Do *you* want to marry him? Do you love him?"

"I think I do. Ummmm." Her eyes dreamed a bit. "Yes, I guess I do!" she finally said.

Then her face clouded, "It's hard though. I'm not sure about how I should act. I feel like I'm playing a part sometimes. Like, I know I'm a woman, but am I a woman in the way other women are? Or am I being myself? Does that sound ridiculous?"

I smiled to reassure her. "I don't think so," I said. "It must be hard to have other people telling you how to be what you now know you are."

"That's it!" she interrupted explosively, punctuating her words with an exasperated grimace and flailing arms, thrown upward in frustration. "I know I'm a woman! I'm even starting to *like* being one! But I don't know *how* to be!"

My goodness, I thought. *You certainly are getting the tantrum part down!* But I said, "You have to take the thing in stages and find your way as you go. The externals, like makeup and how you act, can help direct some of the internals."

"How? I'm not questioning whether you're right. I just want to know how it works."

"Well, take makeup. It isn't going to *make* you more feminine, but it may make you *look* more feminine. And then that may help you link the look with how it feels. Your own femininity has to grow out of who you are, but it can be harder to get in touch with if you look masculine outwardly."

We chatted on, discussing the merits of wearing pearls instead of a chain necklace. She left, but her question stayed with me. How do the seeds we plant help femininity or masculinity "grow" in women and men?

Planting Good Seed: Act by Faith, Feelings Will Follow

Sometimes, in cases of paralysis, a technique called "patterning" is used. This can be effective in by-passing damaged nerve tissue. Instead of the brain giving the signals for things, you have to make the body parts or limbs do those things in the hope that the signals will get back to the brain. In time, the actions might become something the brain itself can direct again instead of the stimulus coming from an outside source. In effect, patterning is planting good seeds in those who are physically paralyzed.

We have to perform a similar process for people paralyzed in their gender identity. Their God-given masculinity or femininity really is there, but they may not be able to reach those attributes.

The "nerves" lying between the identity and its expression have been damaged somehow.

So, we ask God to heal the damage. As He does, we begin, by faith, to act upon His healing by retraining the expression. The ultimate goal is for the expression of femininity or masculinity to become one's own, though initially it may seem contrived.

But is it really contrived? Or is it just a part of the learning process? How can you tell?

As a man or woman begins to experience their true gender and its expression in masculinity or femininity—something that should have happened to them as they passed through puberty—there may be some confusion as to whose feelings they are having. Like Anne, they wonder whether they have merely been programmed or are actually developing their God-given gender identity. Or, like Paul, one young man I know, someone may purposely question the change that has truly taken place, in order to create confusion and consternation.

Planting, Patience, and Productivity

Paul is handsome and smart. He has been out of a gay lifestyle now for several years and will soon be getting married. His heart's desire is to tell young people what he knows about the lies involved in homosexuality.

One day, while speaking to a high school group, an adult woman from the audience challenged his position that homosexuality is not inborn. "How can you say that?" she asked. "For instance, I knew you were gay the moment you walked in. I could tell right away! You just look effeminate."

This hurtful comment had only one purpose: to damage something very precious God was doing in this man's life. If he were your son or brother and you heard this woman reviling him, how would you respond? If you saw that from a pure heart Paul walks daily into this battle to help others make right choices, what would you say to her?

My friend, if you are a Christian, then he *is* your son and your brother and he engages daily in battle in the name of your Lord. Sometimes all he needs is your encouragement to carry on. That night he needed mine. "Mona, do you think I'm masculine?" he asked. "I mean, do you think I look gay?"

The question did not surprise me at all. I have heard the same thing asked repeatedly in different forms—even from people who have been out of homosexuality for years. But before me now sat a young man I loved deeply who really wanted to know if he still had the "look" of a gay man.

It was important that my answer be honest. "Paul, I think you are very masculine. And, no, I don't think you appear gay," I answered truthfully. Then I challenged him: "But why would that be a problem if you did?"

"That wouldn't be good," he said. "I want to be an example to kids."

"Listen, Paul, that woman zeroed in on what she thought was your greatest weakness. She hit the mark pretty close, huh?"

Face flushed, he nodded.

"But our greatest weaknesses are where God has the most ability to be glorified. That woman won't have very much to say if you simply agree that you have a long way to go and move on to the next question or comment. You diffuse her venom.

"More importantly, in the process, you may encourage some kid who thinks that merely struggling in masculinity or appearing less masculine than others is the proof of homosexuality. You show them that masculinity is available to all men. In some it will look different than others. You are masculine because God made you a man. Paul, you *will* develop into what God created you as a man to be while you grow in obedience to what you were created in Christ to be."

Too bad that woman had not also seen Paul about six years earlier with his campy humor, highly affected speech, flittering hand gestures, and color-coordinated hot-pants outfits. The change God had accomplished would have stunned her. But it would come as no surprise to us because he and many other men and women we know had planted for success. "The seed is the word of God. . . . But that on the good ground are they, which in an honest and good heart, having heard the word, keep it, and bring forth fruit with patience" (Luke 8:11, 15).

A Well-Watered Garden: Witnessing to Non-Christian Gays

"WAIT, YOU GUYS," SHE CALLED. "I CAN'T GO AS FAST AS YOU."
Looking up, she watched the backs of her three older sisters as they
bent over their bicycles to pedal up the long, slow hill.

"Just keep coming," the eldest, Ruth, called back breathlessly.
"We'll wait for you at the top."

As she gained the top of the hill they began to push off again.
"Oh, no. Now I get a rest, too," she whimpered. "I'm so thirsty. Do
you think there's anywhere here to get a drink?"

Four pair of eyes squinted in the sunshine. "There's a church
over there," said Becky. "I don't think they're open on Saturdays,
but maybe someone is cleaning or something."

"We can't go to a church," Ruth commanded. "It's only for
Christians and we aren't Christians."

"Do you have to be?" Becky asked. "Maybe they won't know we
aren't. We could just get some water and leave."

"I don't think Daddy would like it if we went there," Bayla
spoke. "Jewish people don't ever go to churches."

But the youngest's whine finally decided it. "I'm so thirsty. I'm
not going any further without something to drink!"

"Come on. I just hope we don't get into any trouble," Ruth said,
taking charge. "Don't go inside!"

They drew their bikes up along the drive to a back door and knocked. The pastor, who was studying for Sunday's message, came and opened the door. There stood four hot, dusty little girls, ranging in age from seven to twelve. He was young and friendly. "Hello," he smiled. "Can I help you?"

Ruth spoke. Remembering it was not proper to say *can*, she asked, "May we have a drink of water?"

I'd have to be made of stone not to know how to respond to that question! he thought. And, bringing several cups of water, he came outside and sat with the girls. As they drank, he told the story of a man named Jesus who, meeting a woman at a well, asked for a drink. "Jesus told her about water for the soul," he said. "When people drink this living water, they're never thirsty again."

Even seven-year-olds know when their souls are dry. The youngest one wanted to hear more, but it was time to go.

"You could have some of this living water if you wanted it," he continued.

I do want it, she thought. "How do you get it?" she asked.

"Uh, we have to go," Ruth said, somewhat apologetically.

"Could you wait for a minute more?" he asked. Taking the seven-year-old's hand, he moved beside her and prayed with her to receive Jesus Christ and, as promised, be filled with living water. Finally, the four girls got back on their bikes and started off down the drive. He waved good-bye and wondered, *Will she follow you, Lord?*

He never saw her again. But though there were several detours along the way, I am still drinking from the well where that kind man led me.

The Heart of Evangelism

This pastor knew evangelism was the art of using situations God presents as opportunities to share His love and truth. He found in the tired little girl a receptive heart. But what about those who do not want to hear the truth, or those who are not receptive to the gospel? How can we respond to the man or woman who does not choose to change and repent of sin?

Men and women involved in homosexuality may be categorized into three basic groups:

- Those with a Christian and/or church background who are often pro-gay in their theological perspective
- Those with no Christian background
- Those who are militant in their homosexuality

These are rough delineations, described simply to suggest possible walls to the gospel and how we, in sharing the healing and salvation Jesus Christ offers, might surmount these barriers. Let us take an extended look at each category, and its unique problems and possibilities.

Those with a Christian/Church Background

First, there are professing Christians and those with a "churched" background. These have either embraced a gay lifestyle and are either unwilling to change or simply do not know if change is possible or how to change. They may even believe homosexual involvement is morally wrong.

I realize many believers encounter a theological problem here. They think *real* Christians cannot knowingly remain involved in sin, or else they were not really Christians in the first place. This is an issue that I frankly refuse to argue. What's important is that *they* think they are Christians. Furthermore, they believe their brand of Christianity allows them to be homosexually involved at the same time.

Our job in reaching out to these is not to judge whether they are saved or not, but *to approach them in whatever way they may be reached.* Is it more important to be right or that they become truly saved and redeemed? God has a fundamental plan for humanity that probably has less to do with theology than with His overwhelming love for people.

This category of gays and lesbians—those who believe they are Christians—might easily be compared with the Samaritan woman who met Jesus one day as described in John's Gospel. She had some spiritual training in her background, and this passage illustrates how Jesus reached her with the truth even when she had given her life over to a lie.

The passage begins with these words: "There cometh a woman of Samaria to draw water: Jesus saith unto her, Give me to drink" (John 4:7).

What is so remarkable about the Lord asking the woman for some water? Look at her response: "Then saith the woman of Samaria unto him, How is it that thou, being a Jew, askest drink of me, which am a woman of Samaria? For the Jews have no dealings with the Samaritans" (John 4:9).

Why is a Jewish man talking with me? she may have wondered. *He asks for a drink! No Jew has ever asked me for anything! Jews all hate Samaritans.* (A professing Christian who chooses a gay lifestyle might give a similar response within the context of a calm conversation with a Christian who believes homosexual activity is sin: *This person disagrees with who I am and what I do. Why's he talking with me?*)

The woman at the well probably experienced Jews' displeasure at some point in her life. Perhaps she had learned to simply stay away from them. Maybe she approached the well that day and, noticing a Jew there, wondered if she should wait until he was gone. We don't really know. But, from her own words, we see her surprise that the Lord would talk with her, much less put Himself in a place of indebtedness to her.

What was Jesus doing?

First, Jesus reached out to the woman in spite of her seemingly unrepentant heart and her attitude of prejudice or, at least, suspicion toward Him. The Lord was not afraid of her sin. Nor was He prejudiced against her. This woman's background and way of speaking with Him did not cause offense. He did not assume she "wouldn't be interested." Jesus was friendly. He extended Himself to people quite freely. What about us?

A good illustration comes from the 1994 Exodus International Conference. There, Mary Heathman tried to reach out to someone in simple friendliness, but her efforts were repulsed. Mary is the mother of a thirty-something daughter and twenty-something son, and also the Executive Director of Where Grace Abounds, a Denver-based ministry to those overcoming homosexuality and to their families.

As it was her job this particular morning to introduce the speakers, she found a quiet spot to confer with the Lord and arrange her thoughts before His throne. A young woman sat down near her and smiled. Mary smiled back. Sadly, her neighbor's smile froze when her gaze encountered Mary's name tag, which declared her association with Exodus. The following is an excerpt from Mary's journal that morning.

> Father, I'm supposed to be introducing Tony, Frank, Ruel, and Esly this morning, and I will. But I sit here across from a young woman who sat down before she saw my name tag, and (now that she sees it) is hostile toward us. I will go and introduce speakers who will share with those who want to hear. Who will speak to this young woman?
>
> She sits here and believes I hate her. She sits here in the presence of love, but she's missing it. Who will let her know she is loved? I smiled and made a comment about her breakfast, but she shut me out. My name tag triggered a false belief. Lord, send someone without a name tag, send someone to love her.

Jesus had the ability to meet people without a name tag on His lapel. If we want to be successful for Him, we must develop this same gift.

Second, the Lord spoke to the woman about her bondage and the need for freedom from bondage.

The Samaritan woman asked Jesus a question, "Why have you, a Jew, asked something of me?"

"Jesus answered and said unto her, If thou knewest the gift of God, and who it is that saith to thee, Give me to drink; thou wouldest have asked of him, and he would have given thee living water" (John 4:10).

She was in bondage to the task of daily drawing water from the local well. Think about it! Water to drink, to wash with, to water livestock with—all had to be carried. Jesus knew how to get her attention!

This might be likened to the concerns all people carry. Our common humanity is often a great starting point to engage a gay or lesbian in conversation. There are similar aspects in life we all must bear. Use those commonalities as a springboard to get acquainted. Like asking for a cup of water, you may disarm the thought that you could not possibly understand anything about that person's life. It certainly engaged the Samaritan woman! "Where does this water come from?" she asked. "You don't have anything to draw with and the well is deep."

"Jesus answered and said unto her, Whosoever drinketh of this water shall thirst again: But whosoever drinketh of the water that I shall give him shall never thirst; but the water that I shall give him shall be in him a well of water springing up into everlasting life" (John 4:13–14).

Then she wanted the water about which the man spoke! "Sir," she said. "Give me this water, that I thirst not, neither come hither to draw" (v. 15). Remember, He started the conversation out by highlighting His own thirst. She never said *she* was thirsty! Jesus said that the water He gives will cause a person to never thirst again. She wanted the water He was talking about. She had become aware of her need.

But Jesus knew that, as great as her physical needs were, this woman was also in bondage through poverty in her spirit. She had no well to draw upon for the water that brings spiritual life. Jesus asked a further request to show her the thirst in her soul: "Jesus saith unto her, Go, call thy husband, and come hither" (John 4:16).

Her answer, that she had no husband, led Jesus to point out her state of sinfulness. She was living with a man who was not her husband, and he was the sixth man she had been with.

How might this apply to the gay or lesbian? Perhaps we can probe to find ways that the promises held out by their own ideal of a gay lifestyle have not been fulfilled. I would suggest this is how Jesus would approach them.

Obviously, unless the Lord opens an extraordinary one-time opportunity to speak with someone gay, earning the right to explore such sensitive areas requires your commitment to an ongoing relationship—just as it would to evangelize someone in any other kind of sin.

Third, after showing her God's grace, Jesus also told her the truth. Even though He might have offended this woman, Jesus pointed out the wrong direction in her life. Was she offended? Maybe. We cannot see her face as Jesus did. Her words tell us she definitely got the point. Moreover, she tried to evade it.

"The woman said unto him, Sir, I perceive that thou art a prophet. Our fathers worshipped in this mountain; and ye say, that in Jerusalem is the place where men ought to worship" (John 4:19–20).

Did you hear Jesus say anything like this? He only said she is not married to the man she is living with and that she has had five husbands before him. What is her purpose in mentioning a place of worship?

Trying to use her lower status as a Samaritan to claim that Jesus is prejudiced against her, she levels an accusation of discrimination against the Lord! (This is a tactic gay individuals often use against Christians to evade the truth as well.) In essence, she says, "There was a time when our (same) ancestors worshiped here. Now your prophets tell us this isn't good enough—we have to worship in Jerusalem" (my paraphrase).

What did Jesus do? He simply sidestepped the controversy entirely and hammered home the truth: She must someday stand before God and give an account. Everything else was a non-issue: being a Samaritan and therefore worshiping Him in the wrong location; her status as a woman; whether things she had set her affections upon had been realized or not. She would stand before God with the fact that she had not responded to His truth and to His Son, who is the Truth. She was living in sin and rejecting the light. That would be the sole basis of God's judgment upon her and that was what Jesus wanted her to see.

Thus, Jesus modeled how to reach out to someone engaged in sin. We should not shun them because of their sinful state or because we are intimidated by them. We should freely offer God's grace. We must never compromise the truth nor allow our perception of it to choke out His love.

Pro-gay Christians and gays with a church background are like the Samaritan woman. They already claim some belief in God's Word, although they may try to change or evade its meaning. They have some type of relationship with God and Jesus. We need to demonstrate God's grace, and in particular show His ability to cleanse and heal when His children turn from their sin. We need to remind them of the truth, that sin is in their lives as long as they continue in homosexuality. Then, I believe, we will see hearts turn back to God in repentance.

Those with No Christian/Church Background

What about people who do not believe in or claim God's truth? This is the second category of people to whom you may witness. These non-Christians are either homosexually oriented, but believe it is wrong, or have embraced homosexuality on some level as a way of life.

Does it matter what these individuals believe about God? Whether they trust in God or His Word makes no difference—someday they will stand before Him in judgment. The horror is that they do not know it!

I saw an example of this type of tragedy one evening as our family drove down Highway 101 between my sister's house in San Francisco and our home thirty minutes to the north in Marin County. Twilight dimmed the hazy Labor Day afternoon. We were full of barbecued hot dogs, salty potato chips, children's games, and good conversation with family.

"Mike! What is that on the road?" I asked in alarm. "Oh, no, someone's dog!" Running uphill into the oncoming traffic, his tongue lolling slightly to one side of his mouth, was an old dog. He seemed oblivious to the traffic whizzing past him and the danger bearing down upon him.

"Can't we stop?" I wailed. "Poor thing! He doesn't even know what's going on. He's going to be killed!"

"I can't stop safely here," Mike replied. "I'm sorry, honey. There isn't anything we can do."

"You could at least try!" I insisted angrily. "How can you just drive on and let him get killed?"

His face set in grim lines, Mike drove on. Sadly, I knew he was right. We could not safely do anything in the dimming light on that crowded highway. So we watched impotently as the dog ran by and into his eternity. After we took everyone home, my son Jonathan and I went back and found him where he lay dead at the roadside.

How I would have loved to have stopped and saved that poor dog! My stomach lurched and churned at the desire to prevent his headlong destruction. The old dog's needless death was sad. But it is only a shadow of the tragedy of men and women all around us, running heedlessly into eternity without God—sometimes because no one has warned them of their danger. And yet, how often I fail to reach out to people around me. What should we do? What can we say?

First and most important, remember that grace and truth are always found in Jesus. Everyone needs salvation. No one can address the wrong in his or her life without first developing a relationship with the only One who has authority to deal with sin. And to expect anyone to change themselves so they may become acceptable for salvation is a false gospel of works. You do not need to point out a person's homosexuality, even if it is glaringly obvious. We all need Jesus simply because we are men and women. Speak to a person on that basis rather than standing in judgment of their particular sin.

Second, remember, grace rains upon all people, not just those whom you or I choose. God's kindness is all-inclusive, complete, and all-encompassing. Our Lord did not die on a cross for this one or that one. He died for all! Nor does He expect us to be selective in our kindness to witness. We carry the good news to all the world, not just the ones we choose. Every man and woman who cross our path should be offered grace and forgiveness. They may not want it, but we should make it available.

Jesus Himself gave the command: "Ye have heard that it hath been said, Thou shalt love thy neighbor, and hate thine enemy. But I say unto you, Love your enemies, bless them that curse you, do good to them that hate you, and pray for them which despitefully use you, and persecute you; That ye may be the children of your Father which is in heaven: for he maketh his sun to rise on the evil and on the good, and sendeth rain on the just and on the unjust" (Matt. 5:43–45).

Jesus expects us to bring His message of hope to everyone because anyone who does not know Jesus and responds to His truth is rushing headlong into their eternity.

Militant Gay and Lesbian Activists

The third group we may have an opportunity to share the good news with consists of the so-called "militant gays" or "gay activists." These terms bring to the evangelical mind all sorts of negative connotations. Militant gays and lesbians vehemently defend their lifestyle and believe they are engaged against Christians and others in a battle for their gay rights.

If we could say that those who choose to be gay but are not militant are rushing past us to destruction like the old dog on Highway 101, then militant gays could be characterized as charging along, biting at everyone who tries to impede their path to ruin. When the militants tend to have such a strong bias (if not hatred) against Christians and Christianity, how can we possibly reach them for the kingdom?

The key principle in presenting truth to such individuals is called "ministering in the opposite spirit." As I sat talking one afternoon with John Smid, director of Love In Action, I was struck anew with the wonder of God's plan for men and women, and our part in it. "How do you reach out to people who are not interested in the gospel message?" I asked.

John smiled. "We have to recognize that we're dealing with someone who struggles with severe rejection. The church's response has often been to reject them further, at least until they straighten out their 'problem.'"

"But that won't happen unless someone breaks through that rejection barricade they've built," I responded.

"Exactly! But remember they didn't build that barricade alone. *They've been rejected all their lives!* So they get caught in a vicious cycle. They may want to change, but they need to get close to others to do so. They act out in various ways which causes people to reject them further."

"When you say 'act out' are you referring to militant gays?" I asked.

He nodded in agreement. "The militant gay is like a cornered animal. So many people are talking at him, he finds it difficult to hear what individual voices are saying. You see, not everyone is saying the same thing."

"That's pretty frustrating if you're just one of the voices," I said. "I've tried sometimes and gotten totally shut out. They just didn't want to hear what I had to say."

"Well, Mona, you need to understand that coming from such an emotional vacuum, they don't realize that some people are not rejecting them."

Now I was really intrigued. "How can you keep from rejecting?"

"I think the secret is that you have to respect them in the same way you do anyone else. Every man and woman is created in God's image, even if they aren't walking as God would want. You don't need to like or agree with their lifestyle, but that shouldn't stop you from treating them with dignity."

"Is that what you mean when you say to 'minister in the opposite spirit'?"

"That's it!" John said, leaning forward excitedly. "You can't expect a person to respond to hostility with anything but hostility. We have to be the peacemakers. We have a message of peace and love from God, so we can't hope to impart that message in hatred and anger."

The Bible states this principle clearly: "A soft answer turneth away wrath: but grievous words stir up anger" (Prov. 15:1); "By long forbearing is a prince persuaded, and a soft tongue breaketh the bone" (Prov. 25:15); "Let your speech be always with grace, seasoned with salt, that ye may know how ye ought to answer every man" (Col. 4:6).

An amazing, living application of these verses occurred early in 1992. Sy Rogers, who serves in Singapore as a missionary for Exodus International, was teaching in Melbourne, Australia. He later reported: "GLAD (Gays and Lesbians Against Discrimination) came to protest my testimony meeting at the Church of Christ. They were led by one of Victoria State's most aggressive and volatile activists.

"Many prayer chains had been activated across Melbourne. After worship, I opened the meeting and asked the Christians there to stand if they felt gays had indeed been discriminated against and mistreated and unloved by the church. Of course, all the Christians immediately stood and I led them in a prayer of repentance, asking forgiveness from God and the gay community. This diffused the tension and created an open atmosphere.

"Even though the protesters didn't agree with all our ideology, they expressed their gratitude to the church leaders for the loving, nonjudgmental attitude of reconciliation presented that night."

Such acts of humility can plow open hard hearts to prepare them for receiving the seed of the gospel. But how often is our position conciliation in truth instead of condemnation or compromise? How many times do we merely respond out of our own fear rather than a true desire to understand and help another? How often do we become the accuser, judging and reviling as our adversary Satan does to us, rather than advocating their cause before the throne of grace as does our Savior?

There is no doubt that the militant gay or lesbian you face is wrong in his or her thinking. But how much of that is your responsibility? Be clear in your own position before God before you approach that person lest you only make things worse. Know what authority God has given His children and what He has not given.

We must remember the mindset of such beleaguered men and women and that fear and rejection have built a barricade into which they have now backed themselves. If we truly seek in God's love to share His gift of life with them, how can we present our offering in a nonconfrontational way? How can we encourage them to investigate the validity of what we say?

These people for whom Christ died are like wanderers in a hot, dry desert. They long for a cool drink and a shady spot to rest. Everything in their lives lends strength to the parching wind that blasts across their existence and robs them of beauty.

What have we to offer? Water! Abundant, flowing water from the Well that never runs dry! Like a beckoning garden within a cool oasis, we can give to a smitten world around us a gift of rest and reparation. It all starts with one glassful of water. Thirsty people want to drink! What stops them? Often, it is our lack of respect.

Remember the name tag that cut the young woman off from Mary Heathman? Though Mary did not have an opening to tell this woman about the living water, God still could use their "chance" encounter when Mary prayed and responded to the woman with respect. The right attitude that Mary exhibited, combined with the name tag, gave that woman a wordless message. That kind of witness is a cool drink of water to a thirsty soul. Most importantly, it is a libation that has a chance of being received, because it is offered with respect.

CHAPTER TEN

Lonely Advocates:
Help for Family Members and Friends

THE OLD MAN LEANED HEAVILY ON THE GATE, GAZING INTO THE disappearing ribbon of road. As he bent his head, the setting sun turned his white hair into a silvery crown. "O Lord God, have mercy on my boy. I know he walked away from You and me at the same time. Please forgive him, God, and bring him back."

"Father?" a voice behind him interrupted. His elder son stood, outlined in the light from the house. "What are you doing out here?"

"I am just watching," the father sighed.

"Father," the son said impatiently, "you need to let go. He isn't coming back."

"I still pray that he will," his elder bristled. Then he said more patiently, "Where are you going, Son?"

"There's still enough light to work in the lower thirty acres. I thought I would do it now while it's cool. Are you going in soon?"

"Shortly. I'll watch a bit more."

"What makes you think he'll ever come back?" the young man ground out through clenched teeth. "It's been years since he left."

The old man smiled slightly, "I can't help it. I miss my boy. Son, you go out to work when you have the opportunity. That's how I pray for your brother—every night that I can, I watch. Maybe God will bring him home."

The Forgotten Wounded

This chapter is about the group of people who are often overlooked when we talk about ministry to those involved in homosexuality. They are the—families and friends—and loved ones of gays and lesbians.

These people know something about the sorrow of separation. They live it when they watch for their children, siblings, and friends caught up in a gay lifestyle. Their pain is often ignored by other Christians for several reasons. First, they do not feel the liberty to talk about their hurt because of prejudice and ignorance in the church against those who are or were involved in homosexuality. They may believe they will be ostracized for their loved one's "unmentionable" sin.

Second, they may feel restricted from getting help at "ex-gay" ministries. Family members are part of a relational pattern that in itself raises an accusation against them. The reasoning is that their children's or siblings' involvement in homosexuality may be, at least in part, a by-product of the way these people related to them. Even though many ministries would help them, their own guilt and fear often get in the way.

Finally, secular people busily try to convince everyone that homosexuality is acceptable. Those who hold the world's standards offer little help for those who hold God's standards.

The church, "ex-gay" ministry, and the world appear to offer little solace to family and friends. And so they keep their lonely watch, like the old man at the gate, lonely advocates praying for that one person God has given them.

The True Advocate

Advocacy originated with God. Throughout the Old Testament, God came to the defense of His chosen people. Even so, not until the death of Jesus on Calvary did humankind fully comprehend the extent of God's commitment to us. Jesus saves any who would turn to Him, repent of the wrong they do, and ask for salvation.

Christ loves each one of us passionately, enough to defend us with His own life. But there is another who hates us with almost the same intensity. Because we were created in the image of God, Satan wants to destroy every man and woman. Like two jurists before the throne of God—one an advocate, the other an accuser—they battle for our souls, and for the soul of that one whom you love.

Look at the cross of Jesus and see the lonely advocate there. When no one understood, He died for those who would rather be accusers than advocates themselves. Though a desolate place, the cross became a tree of life for us. And in like manner, if you are a lonely advocate for someone, God can use the desolation you experience for your loved one to drive you before the throne of life with their case.

These lonely advocates are often on the side of the Great Advocate, but they may not be on the side of His servants here. For that reason, Christians who plead the cause of someone dealing with homosexuality or lesbianism often feel they are treated differently from their fellows in the church. Their situation might be likened to the people of Israel who had family members living "outside the camp."

Outside the Camp

According to Leviticus, in the Israelites' wilderness journey, those who were unclean for any reason remained outside the camp. They were not allowed to participate either in worship or the general life of the encampment. On the perimeter lived lepers and others with disease, and those convicted of crimes died. Burial took place outside the camp, so the corruption of decaying flesh would not be inside. The encampment of God's people was supposed to be a clean, wholesome place.

To live outside the camp was to be in disfavor and shame. And though family members of yours might live inside the camp, enjoying all the blessings of that community, they probably experienced a certain amount of shame at your status. Still, as hard as it was, God's people accepted His judgment for those they loved.

No one was exempt. Miriam, the older sister of Moses, ended up outside the camp because she and her brother Aaron murmured against Moses. Miriam was stricken with leprosy for her part. But she had an advocate: "And Moses cried unto the LORD, saying, Heal her now, O God, I beseech thee" (Num. 12:13). At Moses' request, God did heal Miriam, though she had to remain outside the camp seven days to accomplish the ceremonial cleansing necessary to re-enter.

Miriam's rebellion was against God who rightly judged it. But the Master's servant at times may entreat the Master and receive his request. Here we see the picture of true advocacy. Had she not wronged Moses? Did he not have cause to be angry as the much harangued leader of a very rebellious group? But instead he earnestly brought her case before God.

Many today who rebel against God contract HIV disease while participating in sin. Often compared to leprosy by Christians, AIDS causes people to be ostracized. God may not heal them physically, but our prayer requests on their behalf may help them come back inside the camp spiritually.

If you have a loved one outside the camp, you may be the only one bringing their case to God. How can you go about it? And how can you ensure personal success and spiritual growth as you labor on behalf of someone you care for?

Remain Grafted into the Vine

The deep cold of a January morning in the Sacramento Valley penetrated our fingers and toes as we walked through the kiwi vines of Aunt Shirley and Uncle Frank's farm in Gridley, California.

Every winter after the fruit is picked and the vines are pruned, Frank and Shirley gather the cut branches. Florists buy the naked, supple bracts with their curling tendrils and knobby shapes, and add various decorations to make wreaths.

Walking in the blue-gray haze amongst the cuttings, Shirley and I talked about the family while weaving our wreaths. Here and there we stopped to add in a slender branch, until, at the end of the hour, the decorations were finished.

How flexible the cuttings were in the winter, still half alive with the life of the vine. But how dry and unyielding they became by summer, for, once cut, they began to die. Similarly we are grafted into Christ as a part of His spiritual family, and it is important to abide in that vine: "I am the vine, ye are the branches: He that abideth in me, and I in him, the same bringeth forth much fruit: for without me ye can do nothing. If a man abide not in me, he is cast forth as a branch, and is withered; and men gather them, and cast them into the fire, and they are burned" (John 15:5–6).

The first line of defense for those who advocate is to protect their own position in Christ. We always remain grafted into the vine that is our source of life, but "abiding" depends on obedience. We must never sacrifice our spiritual well-being for the "good" of a loved one. But we can be assured that when we abide, our prayers are heard and answered: "If ye abide in me, and my words abide in you, ye shall ask what ye will, and it shall be done unto you" (John 15:7).

The branch securely attached to its vine is strong and resilient. Everything the vine has, it shares with each branch. But, verse 7 begins with the word "if." We must meet conditions in our lives in order to abide and remain effective prayer advocates for someone in need.

Seek the Lord for Your Own Spiritual Life

Hosea 10:12 says: "Sow to yourselves in righteousness, reap in mercy; break up your fallow ground: for it is time to seek the LORD, till he come and rain righteousness upon you."

Everything in this verse pivots around the word *for*. The first part of the verse advises what must be done *since* it is time to seek God and the righteousness He wants to bring. We seek the Lord by sowing in righteousness, reaping in mercy, and breaking up the fallow ground. Few people have trouble in seeking the pleasures of this world. Yet amazingly, we who were created in God's image and then born again through redemption into His inheritance must be constantly reminded by Him how to look for Him.

If we are engaged in advocacy for another, it is a safe assumption that God has a plan for purifying us as well and quite likely will use the process of our pleading someone else's case. But we can neither plant righteousness nor reap mercy until the field is plowed and prepared for seed. Therefore, the instruction is to break up the fallow ground.

Farmers describe as *fallow* an area that is plowed and either left unplanted or planted in a crop that will merely be plowed under later. Thus, a fallow field has been purified and the nutrients actively replenished. But the activity does not produce a crop; it merely produces a field ready to plant.

How like our Lord to spend such energy on the field! But then, a well-prepared field yields the best crop. God orders the lives of those He calls as advocates that they might be equipped for the arduous task of pleading before His throne. Our Lord knows better than we how difficult a job it is and what is required on our part to do it well.

Love One Another

He stated it plainly: "This is my commandment, That ye love one another, as I have loved you" (John 15:12).

That ye love. That is the big secret! If love is not growing in us, we are not growing in Him. That flow of love is the very life of the vine we were grafted into. To love in the same way Jesus loved us is to remain firmly attached to the vine and simultaneously extend our love and prayers to those around us.

But Jesus' love for us is a tough kind. It demands that our old sinful nature and its acts die with Him on that cross. It expects purity. If we would love one another in the way we are loved, we must expect nothing less than that same holiness. Though we love someone and advocate for them before God, we can never compromise our biblical standard of righteousness or run ahead of our King.

Consider Carefully How You Witness

A question that is often asked in various forms is, "How should I witness to my loved one?"

The fairest answer I can give is this: I do not know. Like most things, because we deal with individuals we have to individualize the way we treat them. A good rule of thumb to use is that you'll know the tree by its fruit.

If you have tried something and your loved one withdraws emotionally, you may not be taking the right approach or it may not be the right time. This is where prayer can save the day. By taking the time to pray carefully beforehand, you will less likely rush in and do the first thing that comes to mind. And, of course, God knows the right approach for each individual. But to find out what He knows, we have to ask. And sometimes He only says, "Wait."

But at times God will give you peace about sharing a timely message—and that will bear fruit. I experienced such a situation beginning the day my mother died in a house fire. The call came so early in the morning that I barely had time to throw on some clothes and race down the highway to the town where she lived. When I arrived, the scene was pure pandemonium. Fire trucks from five different companies were there. Thick hoses up and down the street poured water into the smoking structure.

Bright yellow tape across the road forbade my entry. "That's my mother's house," I pointed, ducking under the tape and striding past a challenging policeman. The entire block was sealed off. It seemed to take forever to walk the familiar block. Where was my brother, Morris, who had called me? Where was my sister, Bayla, who had been in the fire? And why, oh why, hadn't my mom gotten out?

Suddenly a young man appeared. "Mona?" he asked.

"Yes, who are you?" I returned somewhat rudely.

"I'm John, Susan's brother," he answered. "This is my friend Carl. We've been watching for you. We'll take you to Morris."

As he took my elbow and led me gently through the crowd, I tried to understand who he was. Finally it came to me. This was my sister-in-law's brother, John, visiting from the East. By the time I understood, we had reached my brother and John quietly left us alone.

I think he and Carl were at the funeral and spent some time before finally leaving for their home in the East. Beyond that, I had very little interaction with them. But his act of compassion compelled me to be an advocate for him when I learned that John was dying of AIDS.

First, I asked God if I could write to him and what I should say. "Tell him the truth," was the answer.

Then I asked his sister. "I think he'd love to hear from you, and I don't think he'd be offended," she told me.

Then I asked him. "Dear John . . . " I wrote and told him how his gracious intervention in a difficult time for me helped. I asked if I could bring a message that I thought would encourage him.

It was a long letter. But he read the whole thing and thanked me for it. I don't know how he responded to what I told him, but I am sure he heard the truth about salvation.

Stand on the Promises

When I was fourteen, my father received a huge trophy. It was over two feet high from its gleaming wooden base to the exultant statuette atop the giant loving cup. The brass plate was engraved:

Sol Stoumen
Fighter for Freedom
Fifteen Years

The men who had given the trophy were grateful to my dad for his years of court battles to protect the civil rights of lesbians and gays. He did this at a time when there was no gay rights movement and nearly no advocates on their behalf.

But my father only knew he had lost his case. His business of more than fifteen years ended along with his last court battle. The state of California had won, and they finally closed The Black Cat Cafe, Daddy's gay bar, for good. He put the trophy in a dark cupboard the day he got it. At the same time, Sol Stoumen ended contact with many of the friends associated with the cafe. He also lost much of the joy in his life.

As his daughter, I watched him struggle through the next two decades until his death. As a Christian, I prayed, longing to see him give his life to Jesus and find help.

There was no way to witness to Daddy. He forbade us to tell him anything about our beliefs. All I could *do* was pray. But years after his bar closed, he was dying and came to live with my family. I prayed for the fulfillment of God's promises.

Lord, I've followed You and trusted You. You've put me in this family and given me a father who only knows You as Jehovah. How can I show him Jesus? Couldn't You just heal him? Then he would believe.

I'm not going to heal him,
but if you will fight for him you'll see My salvation in his life.

I'll fight for him. Tell me what to do.

You have to go toe-to-toe with the devil.
Bring your father before Me in prayer
and bring your life before Me as well.
Let Me work on you and let him watch.

For six months, that is what we did. Daddy lived with us while dying of lung cancer. And I fought and grieved, suffering under the unexpected blow of my mother's death in the house fire. At times I wondered at the pain we walked through. But all the while, my father watched.

Finally, just weeks before his death, he concluded there was something different about my husband and me. "Furthermore," he admitted, "the difference may just be Jesus." The day before he died, he asked Mike to come to the hospital and talk to him about the Lord. Then they prayed together.

The promises of God are a rock solid foundation upon which to stand. When you fight with the devil over one you love, you can win with the Rock beneath you.

Enlarge the Borders of Your Tent

The prophet Isaiah gave this directive: "Enlarge the place of thy tent, and let them stretch forth the curtains of thine habitations: spare not, lengthen thy cords, and strengthen thy stakes" (Isa. 54:2).

One day Mike and I took the children to the local mall for dinner. While we were eating, I noticed a man sitting nearby and watching us. The expression in his bloodshot eyes was sorrowful, his wrinkled and dissipated face wore a frown. "Michael, I'm going to go and sit with that man for a few minutes," I said.

"Honey, what are you doing?" Mike challenged my wisdom.

"I think God wants me to encourage him," I insisted. And I went.

"May I join you?" I asked, pausing in front of his table.

His surprise turned to pleasure as he half arose and invited me to sit. "That's a beautiful family you have there," he said.

"Thank you," I replied. "We're very proud of them." Then I asked, "What about you?"

"What about me?" he answered gruffly. "I have no children now." And then he began to cry. "I had a son. A good boy too. But he got called up and sent to Vietnam. I loved that boy, so I joined up and got into the same outfit. Thought I could protect him, but he got killed and I had to come home alone."

"I'm so sorry. You must have loved him very much."

"Didn't do no good," he sniffed. "He's gone and I'm here. I crawled into a bottle and I've been there ever since."

"God can give you other sons," I said. "There are lots of young men who need fathering."

"Nope," he said, shaking his grizzled head. "It's too late for me."

Every so often I see him sleeping on a bench. I keep praying.

If God has allowed you to experience loss like this man, then surely He has a good purpose for your pain. I do not say that lightly. I believe God does let things happen in our lives that appear to be crushing, and yet I know that, but for the forge, the metal would not be strong. It cannot be pleasant in the forge, but it is needful.

As we live, hurts and even disasters will come our way. How will we let them be used? Certainly the deepest trials are always used. Will we give them back to our God and seek His face? Or will we turn from Him and allow the devil to further damage us by robbing even the faith we have in our Heavenly Father?

This is a hard thing to write. Job lost all his children in one blow. But worse, he stood in danger of losing his friendship with God and his opportunity be used by the Lord. If one you love is now gone, step closer to God, enlarge your tents, and look for an orphan who needs your love.

Become a Builder of "Waste Places"

In the spring of 1994, Love In Action's live-in program marked its first-ever family weekend. Family members came from all over the country to attend classes, meet others like themselves, attend church, and generally get new insight into what the young men they loved were doing. Mothers, fathers, sisters, and brothers learned firsthand of the struggles, pain, victory, and joy that come with a walk such as these men had undertaken. And in some instances, participants were also afforded a closer look at their own past to better understand the forces that had helped to misshape their lives.

During this weekend, I talked with the group about the importance of supporting their family members in the difficult task they had begun: walking away from homosexuality. Looking into faces I had never seen before, I saw deep grief and shame banished, replaced by healing and empathy.

For the adult children had not been the only damaged lives touched. Parents and siblings, who had often succumbed to generational defilements or merely the lack of understanding in right relationships, began learning how to bridge the gaps in their families. Together at the foot of the cross, all saw God's amazing power to heal and forgive in our broken families.

By helping these loved ones of the men in the live-in program, Love In Action's staff acted as rebuilders of desolate emotional and spiritual places in people's lives. They would follow Isaiah's instruction: "And they that shall be of thee shall build the old waste places:

thou shalt raise up the foundations of many generations; and thou shalt be called, the repairer of the breach, the restorer of paths to dwell in" (Isa. 58:12).

Those who advocate for their homosexual loved ones are engaged in building waste places. It is hard work, but God's Word promises that in the process, they will repair the breaks in relationships and restore places upon this earth to dwell together. Even foundational, generational breaks will be restored by God's intervention.

Do Not Become an Unwilling Advocate

Not everyone whom God calls wants to be an advocate. Jonah the prophet is perhaps the strongest example of this. When God told Jonah to go and preach to the city of Nineveh, the prophet instead booked passage on a boat to Tarshish. God knew what His servant was about and sent a storm to trouble the boat until eventually Jonah ended up thrown overboard and swallowed by a great fish.

Jonah then cried out to God from within the fish, and the Lord caused him to be vomited up onto land. Then the God of second chances repeated the instructions: "Arise, go unto Nineveh, that great city, and preach unto it the preaching that I bid thee" (Jonah 3:2).

You might think Jonah would have learned his lesson; surely now he would serve the Lord wholeheartedly! But that was not the case. Though obedient *to* God, Jonah was not abiding *with* God. Oh, he did what was commanded, but only out of duty. His heart was not engaged in God's will. So, though he preached the word given him and an entire city repented, Jonah became very angry. "And he prayed unto the LORD, and said, I pray thee, O LORD, was not this my saying, when I was yet in my country? Therefore I fled before unto Tarshish: for I knew that thou art a gracious God, and merciful, and slow to anger, and of great kindness, and repentest thee of evil. Therefore now, O LORD, take, I beseech thee, my life from me; for it is better for me to die than to live" (Jonah 4:2–3).

Poor Jonah. He felt so ill-used. This hapless prophet brought God's message of destruction to Nineveh only to see his worst fears realized. The entire city repented and was spared! How irritating!

Sulking in the little booth he had built for himself outside the city, Jonah's only comfort was a gourd vine God caused to grow over him to provide shade from the sun. But the next day, the Lord caused a worm to kill the vine. Now the prophet sat in the hot wind and fierce sun. He despaired of life itself. What was wrong? He had done what God wanted. Then why did he not have any joy? Why was God not blessing him?

A better question would be: How could God possibly bless one who stood so opposed to the spirit of His divine directives? If God's man cannot bring God's message, who will? There were thousands of people in Nineveh whom the Lord loved unselfishly. He wanted them saved.

The problem was that Jonah did not love them, nor was he willing to let God's love flow through his life to them. Yes, he carried out God's instructions, but his heart was not engaged in God's will.

If we merely carry out the orders of our Lord without regard to His purposes, we miss entirely the true joy of serving God. And we miss blessings promised to those called according to His purpose (see Rom. 8:28). We stop abiding and simply serve for lack of any other calling. That kind of service will soon become very dry and dull. We will begin to wonder where the exciting and victorious Christian life went!

Do Not Become Obsessed

Can we carry things too far? What do we need to consider as we serve as advocates for ones we love?

First, we are not meant to go outside the camp ourselves. Jesus alone was able to go outside to bring others in. Nor should we ever stand with those who oppose our God. In the rebellion of Korah, Moses warned the people as God directed him. "And he spake unto the congregation, saying, Depart, I pray you, from the tents of these wicked men, and touch nothing of theirs, lest ye be consumed in all their sins" (Num. 16:26).

How does this apply to lonely advocates? They must not condone sin.

Second, we are not meant to become obsessed with the loved one for whom we advocate. Parents who plead for their children often become so enmeshed in their prayer requests for that person that they overlook the good the Lord may be accomplishing through apparently bad things.

None of us wants to see those we love hurting. But sometimes that is exactly what it takes for them to see their spiritual poverty.

God has a plan! He loves them more than we do! But He knows what it will take to bring them to repentance. If we intervene and stop the process, we may merely help them stop just short of surrender to God.

Winning Our Case

Peggy has prayed diligently for her daughter for many years. What has been the result of her hours of prayer?

"It's gotten worse and worse," she said. "The more I pray, the deeper in sin she gets."

"Do you ever think, *I just can't go on any more. I don't care?*" I asked.

"Well, yeah. Everybody wants to give up sometimes. But we don't really know what's happening, do we? Appearances can be deceiving. I have to keep praying until God answers me. That may not be until I stand in front of Him in heaven."

Like a lawyer carrying a case through many appeals, this persevering mother has learned that patient endurance in prayer will win the case. She is like the persistent widow who finally received her request, though she pled before an unjust judge. How much more shall we who bring our case before the Righteous Judge? In the words of Jesus: "And shall not God avenge his own elect, which cry day and night unto him, though he bear long with them?" (Luke 18:7).

Or like the old man, watching at the gate, when no one else believes he will ever see his prodigal son again?

Darkness was beginning to obscure his view of the road. "Maybe my son is right and I am foolish to watch, Lord." With that, his face set in stern lines and he began to turn away. "But I'll come back every day until he returns."

As he spoke, the dim form of a traveler appeared far off down the road. Squinting, he peered into the shadows. "Is it him? No, surely too old. . . . Poor man, look how he walks. My son is proud and upright. And this man's so gaunt. This fellow could use a good meal." With that thought, he opened the gate and started toward the stranger.

But something in the look of the other man caused his heart to quicken. It was the one he hoped to see! Running to his son, he hugged him and kissed his neck. His joy rang out, "For this my son was dead, and is alive again; he was lost, and is found" (Luke 15:24).

There is hope.

A Christlike Response to AIDS

CHAPTER ELEVEN

AIDS in the Church:
An Introduction to the Impact of HIV

THIS WAS NEVER INTENDED TO BE A BOOK FOCUSING ON AIDS. However, if you are relating with people who have homosexual issues, sooner or later HIV becomes a relevant topic.

Since many excellent resource materials on AIDS exist now and space here is limited, I will touch on three select issues[1] and refer you to resource organizations which can provide more details. Here are the three essential topics:

+ Who has AIDS, and what is it like? Putting a human face to this isolating epidemic takes HIV disease out of the hypothetical and shows it as a spiritual family matter.

+ Is AIDS God's judgment on homosexuals? If so, would you be interfering with God's plan by helping someone who has AIDS?

+ What basic ways can a local church respond to those affected?

AIDS—A Spiritual Family Affair

"How many people here know someone who has AIDS?" the teacher, Jonathan Hunter, asked. Although well over half of the eighty-member audience raised their hands, I was not among them. "How many have a family member with AIDS?" A dozen hands went up.

"Now, you don't have to answer this next question unless you want to. How many have AIDS themselves or are HIV-positive?" Four courageous men raised their hands.

Scanning the audience slowly, Jonathan continued, making sure to meet our eyes with his. "I know you're all Christians here at this training conference. I want to remind you that I'm a Christian too, and I'm infected with the virus that causes AIDS. So every one of you can leave this room today knowing you *do* have a family member with AIDS—because I'm your spiritual brother in Christ."

As a collective gasp escaped the audience, Jonathan's words hit me full force: If one member is *infected*, the whole family is *affected*, whether that one is a part of the natural, physical family or the spiritual, church family. The next day, I would meet Bob Winter, about whom Mona writes in chapter 15. Finally I would have two human faces to this isolating illness. Soon I would have more. No longer would AIDS statistics be mere numbers; they would represent real people.

At the conference, I learned it would be practically impossible for me to "catch" HIV from casual or social contact with someone infected. And I discovered that regardless of fears I might have about ministering to a person with AIDS, I was not relieved of my responsibility. Later I would read in a book on AIDS, "Courage is fear that has said its prayers." Jesus valued me enough to leave the comforts of heaven, say His prayers in Gethsemane, and die that I might live. How could I ignore the needs of others solely for fear of protecting my own life? Yes, all this confirmed to me my need to become directly involved. After all, is that not the reason why I had come to the training?

During an informal lunch the next day, Bob shared his testimony of spiritual lessons God had taught him through his suffering with AIDS. "I can't stop growing as a Christian just because I'm terminally ill," he told us. Then he talked about how he needed to deal with his emotions rather than suppress them; how he was learning to address grief his family and friends were feeling and to talk openly; how he needed to continue building his relationship with God, because there was no way to predict when the Lord would call him home. *Hmm . . . people with AIDS are no different from the rest of us,* I thought. *AIDS doesn't change their need to grow; it just makes it more of a reality.*

Bob communicated from a heart full of desire to minister the good news and hope to others infected with deadly HIV. There he was, exhausted from battling nausea and a 102-degree fever all day. It was a risk for him to be there: He was actually more vulnerable to catching an illness from us than we were of catching anything from him. But he carried on anyway.

Later, I had the opportunity to talk with Bob one-on-one. "Hope you don't mind if I sit down," he sighed.

"I appreciated what you said about things you've learned, Bob." *He looks so tired, Lord. Please give Him your strength!* "You helped me get a better perspective on what living with AIDS is like."

We chatted just a few minutes. "Time to go," he groaned, pushing himself to the limit just to stand up. I spontaneously reached out and shook hands with him. Bob Winter was the first person with full-blown AIDS I ever met or touched—and I did not even consciously realize that fact until months later. He was just a Christian brother I admired. It was natural to want to shake his hand and thank him for sharing his life.

The Lord used Jonathan and Bob to touch me in a profound way. Both men deeply impressed me with their love for the Lord, honesty in sharing their life stories, and willingness to minister to others.

Back in the early 1980s, I had heard about AIDS and thought, *Oh, Lord! That stuff's awful. Someone should do something about this!* Now I knew I was one of the someones He was inviting to get involved. But that conference showed me that HIV does not exactly have a "learning curve." It's more like a "learning cliff"! If the Lord wanted me to be one of the someones to make a difference, I knew I needed training—a lot more training. And I would need to acquaint myself with those not only *infected* by HIV, but also those *affected*—family members and friends of those with HIV disease. I would like to introduce you to some of the people I have met— because we are all part of the same family.

Dennis Turner

When I met Dennis, he had only been a Christian six months. He had AIDS-Related Complex (ARC), which is halfway between merely being infected and having what is called full-blown AIDS. Dennis experienced typical ARC symptoms: drastic weight loss of over thirty pounds in two weeks, fevers, chills, and profuse night sweats. He developed full-blown AIDS in March of 1990. For a while, he wrote materials for people with AIDS and encouraged those in ministry.

Dennis' health continued to deteriorate. Shortly before his death, I saw him featured in the Jeremiah Films video, *No Second Chance*. There lay Dennis in a hospital bed, IV tubes stuck into his arms, oxygen flowing through breathing tubes in his nose. His weight was gone; his eyes and cheeks were sunken into cavities of gray. He looked like a survivor of Auschwitz. "I'd rather be dying of AIDS and have the relationship I have with Jesus Christ," he said, "than be in perfect health and not know Him at all." Dennis passed into the presence of his beloved Savior just months later. How many other men and women will the Lord snatch from the jaws of eternal death by getting their attention with AIDS?

Sheila Riley

At another AIDS ministry training conference, I met Sheila. Petite, pretty, and spunky, she was the first HIV-positive woman I encountered. You would never have known she carried HIV unless she told you.

We had to do a simulation exercise about getting news from our doctor that we had a terminal illness, would only live six more months, and would gradually get worse. What did we feel at that news? How would we spend our final six months? How would we tell our loved ones?

Sheila had never really considered such questions. I guess she was in denial about her disease. But this small-group exercise cracked her shell of self-protection. As she told the entire group her thoughts, she completely broke down. "I've been HIV-positive for a while," she sobbed, "but I . . . I've never thought about my dying. And now I know I've got to get my life straight with the Lord."

Did I pity her? No. I admired her for seeing the spiritual urgency in her situation. I had already faced some of that kind of shock, pain, and resolve in my own life. Suffering from a debilitating chronic intestinal illness, I never expected to live to see thirty—but I had. In some small way, God showed me I could use my own experiences as a base to empathize with those having HIV disease.

In fact, if we look for them, we can all find such reference points in our own personal history and discover that the HIV/AIDS experience is not as foreign as we first think. Perhaps we have had a long-time interest in healthcare issues or being an advocate for those with no political voice. Maybe a family member experienced a difficult illness or a loved one has died and we know what grief is about. Or we have been given the runaround by government officials who resist giving services that we or a family member need. What is so different between that and AIDS? As we come to know people with HIV disease, we will find that in most ways, they are exactly like us, with many of the same struggles we have.

Jim and Patty

After this conference, I met Jim and Patty, and their two-year-old daughter Jodi—the first child with AIDS I ever met. Patty's first husband lied to her when she confronted him about her suspicions of his IV drug use. Through intimate contact, he had already infected her, but she had no clue because she had no symptoms. He died a few months after their divorce became final, but she had already met and married Jim. Jodi was born infected and, as is typical for infants with HIV disease, quickly developed full-blown AIDS.

Several times I held Jodi in my arms. That long, thin face framed by fair blonde hair etched itself into my memory. I seldom heard her laugh heartily. Her haunting smile always betrayed a hint of her chronic physical pain. *How can this happen to children, God?* I wondered repeatedly.

Last time I saw Patty, she was almost like an Alzheimer's patient—losing her train of thought in mid-sentence and doing bizarre things. Clearly, AIDS-related dementia was setting in as HIV attacked her nervous system directly. She ran away with Jodi and divorced Jim against his wishes. I wonder, *Is Patty in heaven with her Savior even as I write this?* Jodi died before she turned four. Jim was heartbroken by both of the women in his life leaving him, but there were not many people he could talk with about it.

It seems common for individuals affected by AIDS to feel choked by a code of silence which does not allow them to admit they or a family member has AIDS. As I get to know other families affected by HIV disease, I find many have been made outcasts by their churches when they revealed they or a family member had AIDS. They were not encouraged to share their fears or feelings. Instead, they were shunned.

AIDS is a disease that can bring a sense of uneasiness just talking about it. But when you have real, human faces to associate with HIV, it is not so hard to give their human bodies a hug that says, "I love you, brother. I love you, sister."

Also, AIDS ministry is not easy to maintain. It drains the heart at times. But the Lord pours out His blessings, too, such as hearing that someone with AIDS you shared the gospel with has become a Christian. Not only that, he also shared the good news with all eight other patients in the AIDS ward, with six of them likewise giving their lives to the Lord. Those who know they are dying think about eternal issues. People with AIDS constitute another waiting harvest for the church.

All our stories are as varied as God's grace, but we are all family in Christ. To echo Jonathan Hunter's words, "So every one of you can leave . . . today knowing you *do* have a family member with AIDS" because some of them are your spiritual brothers and sisters in Christ."

Is AIDS God's Judgment?

We absolutely must address the serious question of whether AIDS is God's specific judgment on homosexuals. If a person believes it is, then would not helping those with AIDS constitute going against God's hand of carrying out judgment?

An entire book could be written on this question. Probably the best, most detailed presentation on the issue comes from *The AIDS Epidemic: Balancing Compassion and Justice* by Glenn Wood and John Dietrich. They define God's *specific judgment* and then contrast it with other judgments.

> Specific divine judgment in the Bible occurs when God directly intervenes to punish a specific group of people. . .
>
> How does specific divine judgment differ from the universal and cause-and-effect judgments? First, specific divine judgment is directed toward a specific group of people at a specific time for a specific act of rebellion against God or for their innate wickedness. For example, at the time of the flood, "The LORD saw how great man's wickedness on the earth had become, and that every inclination of the thoughts of his heart was only evil all the time" (Gen. 6:5).
>
> Second, specific divine judgment is announced by God himself or by his prophets. . . . Moreover, all specific divine judgments are announced before the judgment begins. The judgment might last for an extended time, as Israel's forty years of wandering or the two and a half years of drought announced by Elijah, but these punishments were proclaimed at the first so that the origin of the judgment was understood . . .
>
> Third, in the Bible's specific divine judgments, the relationship between the sin and the destruction that follows is not cause and effect; rather than the natural consequences of their actions, the unexpected occurs. God causes something out of the ordinary to happen as a signature of his divine wrath.[2]

Some examples of "signature events" include the flood, the nation of Israel wandering in the wilderness forty years while the entire older generation died, God's order to destroy the Caananite peoples, and His pledge to wipe out Ninevah—which was set aside for a time when they repented.

Is AIDS God's judgment on homosexuals? After much consideration, I concluded that AIDS is not a specific judgment on homosexuals or any other group. There are some provocative points in favor of this conclusion:

First, a specific judgment wipes out a class of people entirely, not just some in a hit-and-miss fashion. Therefore, if AIDS were God's judgment on homosexuals, then all homosexuals should get AIDS. In fact, some homosexual men who have had hundreds of partners have not gotten infected, while some with few or even one partner have.

And remember how Christ said that those who looked lustfully at a woman had already committed adultery in their hearts? (See Matt. 5:27–28.) Since, according to Jesus, the thought is as bad as the act, you would expect all men who merely toyed with a homosexual thought to contract HIV also. But they have not.

For a long period, the AIDS epidemic did not reach the lesbian community. How could AIDS be God's judgment on homosexuals when lesbians were excluded? (Although AIDS has now entered this community—as of this writing, at least four cases have been documented in the USA of women contracting HIV by lesbian sexual practices—still that leaves tens of thousands of lesbians untouched directly by HIV.)

Second, if AIDS were God's judgment on homosexuals, why are other types of people affected, such as hemophiliacs, children born to infected mothers, and spouses of IV drug users? And, third, why, in Africa, are mostly heterosexuals afflicted with HIV?

To hold to a position that AIDS is God's judgment on homosexuals requires sidestepping some significant evidence to the contrary. I am *not* saying there is no judgment involved in AIDS, because there are consequences to any action we take which God declares a sin. But to say AIDS is a specific judgment goes far beyond what the facts support.

I believe that much of what motivates an extreme AIDS-equals-God's-judgment opinion is an unrighteous need to place blame on someone, fear and disgust of homosexuals, overconcern about becoming infected, and plain old apathy or not wanting to get personally involved.

If AIDS were around in Jesus' time, I am sure He would have befriended those infected. He would have shown concern and done something for them. And undoubtedly Christ would have balanced compassion with righteousness. Just as He did with the woman caught in adultery (John 8:3–11), Christ would counteract both legalistic and liberal attitudes by accepting and loving people with AIDS, despite how they contracted the HIV virus—while not condoning any of their sins that may have led to this state.

As Christ's representatives on earth, let us seek to act in compassion without compromise toward those affected by HIV.

Corporate Ministry and the HIV Epidemic

Are people infected or affected by HIV disease welcome at your church? Or is your church "HIV-negative"? I believe your answers serve as a barometer on how relevant your local congregation is in ministering to today's culture. In fact, if your local church can deal with the issue of AIDS from a biblically balanced perspective of compassion and holiness, it can deal with just about any other problem that comes along. If it cannot or will not deal with AIDS, you must consider if your church is being obedient to all God calls us to be and to do as the Body of Christ.

These are very strong statements. But then, AIDS is one of the biggest challenges and opportunities the church has faced in its entire history. Why? To deal effectively with AIDS, you must address a host of other issues that tend to make Christians very uncomfortable—and some understandably so. These range from the political to the personal, from the theological to the ethical, from the relational to the eternal. Such as caring about people at high risk of infection: sexually active teens, IV drug users, homeless people, victims of rape, people living in poverty, married couples with one infected partner.

And then come the realizations that sooner or later, if your church reaches out to a variety of people, you will definitely find someone with HIV disease. So, better to consider such issues now, before a crisis hits and potentially irreversible damage is done to the reputation of Christ because your church was not ready.

Becoming and remaining a relevant church means work. But if leaders and congregation can negotiate their way through the apparent obstacles, two marvelous prizes await at the finish line—the eternal salvation of souls and a testimony of Christian integrity with right beliefs *and* right behaviors.

Here is an overview of key areas for church leaders and members to consider. This material is directed primarily to people in church leadership positions, since it is their responsibility to initiate biblically based, medically sound approaches for addressing congregational needs, including those who are affected by HIV/AIDS. (If you are not in a position of responsibility, do not skip the rest of this chapter. You will find here specific prayer concerns to support your leaders!)

Develop an Infectious Disease Policy Statement

An infectious disease policy statement is an informed, unified collection of written hygiene guidelines expected of church workers and congregation members, and a statement of biblical philosophy behind having such a set of policies. It is an "infectious disease" statement instead of just an HIV policy, because the procedures it establishes extend to any contagious illness that may cause people concern.

Why develop a church policy statement on HIV/AIDS and other infectious diseases? I can think of at least four good reasons:

+ You may already have someone with HIV in your church or someone who has a loved one with HIV. A formal infectious disease policy statement reassures them they can share openly their needs without fear of being expelled from the fellowship.

+ If you do not have a policy and someone affected attends your church, your church may split because the congregation has not yet been educated, and some may function out of presumptions and fear instead of accurate knowledge and love.

✦ Part of your testimony in the non-Christian community is to show that Christians care about people struggling with today's social problems. Moody Memorial Church in Chicago ended up with a public relations fiasco when, in the early 1990s, they had not yet finished their infectious disease policy statement and asked an infected youngster to refrain from attending Sunday School for a time. News organizations found out, the American Civil Liberties Union threatened to sue, and the church reinstated the child. The damage control did not stop the church's name from being dragged through the media mud, and the name of Christ and Christians along with it.

✦ It is a means of educating church leaders and congregation members on facts about HIV, the strong evidence against casual transmission, and a biblical, Christlike response to people affected.

Though this policy development and education process may seem tedious, remember the benefits you can reasonably expect from it—a more knowledgeable leadership team and congregation, opportunities to face fears and develop compassion for those in need, a more hygienic church environment for everyone, and an openness towards people with various problems—AIDS-related or not. It does not necessarily mean that you have to or will develop an AIDS ministry, though that is one potential by-product. It may just mean a willingness on the part of people to befriend someone affected by HIV. Let God unfold to your congregation as individuals and as a corporate body that which would please Him.

Welcome People Affected by HIV Disease

According to Revelation 5:9, integrity in ministering the gospel in word and deed involves openness to people of every nation, tongue, tribe, and family. We are called upon to care about all people and to share the good news with them. But how can we accomplish this Great Commission task if we close our hearts and our church to any individual or group?

Many people with HIV become very open to spiritual matters. They know their time is short. This is an opportunity to show God's love and concern for them as people and for their eternal destinies. Likewise, the knowledge that a loved one has a potentially terminal illness may cause family and friends to seek spiritual answers for their own lives.

Offer Basic Assistance

If we want to, we can find many different ways to become involved in ministry to people infected or affected by HIV, all as diverse as our spiritual gifts and personal interests. These are some ways:

+ Behind-the-scenes work in an organization dedicated to AIDS ministry, including clerical support and prayer.

+ Ministry involving interpersonal relationships. You could visit hospital patients with AIDS. Or be a "buddy," visiting one person with AIDS on a regular basis, becoming a friend, and helping with incidental chores that they are no longer able to do.

+ Sharing material goods, such as donating to an HIV food bank, opening your home to family members who travel to your town to visit their loved one, and supporting AIDS ministries financially.

+ Sharing technical knowledge or skills, like expertise and services in counseling, crisis intervention, dental care, employment search help, health care, legal assistance, nutritional counseling, personal business affairs planning, speaking skills, and writing skills.

Let your unique ministry flow from who God has made you to be using your gifts, abilities, and experience.

Nurture an In-Church HIV Ministry

You may have a core group with a special burden for people affected by HIV disease. If so, your church may want to establish an official HIV ministry. Pray, work, and see exactly what kind of "personality" the Lord is developing for this new work. And remember that much of its character depends on the unique gifting of those called to its leadership.

In fact, there is no standard menu of services you must offer in order to qualify as a ministry to people affected by HIV. So far, I have identified about sixty distinct types of services that range from spiritual support to personal support and involvement, from medical/health care to material assistance and benevolence, from technical support to education and training. (For a listing of these services, see the resource section for the Christian AIDS Services Alliance address, and request their application form.)

One note of caution: Start with one or two services that require personal interaction with people who have HIV disease, but less commitment than something like hospice work. For instance, start by helping with errands or trips to the doctor or delivering meals or having hospital visits with those who give permission. If God raises up the people, the money, the time, and the place, then consider higher-commitment work. If not, you will still be doing valuable work that displays God's care and concern for those whom He created.

May we all come to the same ministerial boldness seen in two apostles when they preached after Pentecost. Acts 4:13 states that Israel's leaders marveled, "and they took knowledge of them, that they had been with Jesus." If we see AIDS from God's point of view, the world can see Jesus in the process.

CHAPTER TWELVE

Basic Medical Overview: The Five Questions Most Asked about AIDS

CHURCH PEOPLE WANT TO KNOW THE TRUTH ABOUT HIV. AND I believe they deserve honest, frank responses.

Young people—including Christian youth—especially want to hear real-world answers to their concerns. They have asked my speaker friends in all seriousness and explicitness whether you could contract HIV from your father sexually molesting you, whether using condoms really constitutes "safe sex," about the risks of having oral sex and the dangers of sharing hypodermic needles for shooting steroids. You name it; it's been asked.

I have participated in question-answer panels on HIV for groups of junior high students, high schoolers, Christian college students, and general congregations in churches. Five basic questions keep coming up about HIV/AIDS, so I want to address them. But first there are two most important points to remember about HIV and AIDS. One is medical and the other is ministerial.

First, it is important to know accurate medical facts about what HIV is, how it is transmitted, and what it does to a person's immune system. But even more crucial is to have a biblically sound approach for ministering to the needs of people infected by HIV. If the AIDS virus were transmitted by casual social contact—and there is solid evidence it is not—that still would not negate our responsibility as believers in Jesus Christ to reach out to those who are afflicted.

Second, the key point on modes of transmission to remember is this: There is good evidence that HIV is not transmitted by casual contact, but primarily by one of the four major non-exotic routes of transmission, involving blood contact with contaminated body fluids:

+ Sexual intercourse

+ Sharing hypodermic needles

+ Blood transfusion, blood products, or organ transplants (rarely)

+ Breast milk (rarely)

We should examine medical issues related to HIV disease, and a few basic action points on how Christians can use this information for prayer and ministry.[1] Presented here are the most important details and examples. If you desire further information on HIV or precautions in caring for someone infected, contact some of the referral organizations found in the resource section of this book.

1. What Do the HIV and AIDS Terms Mean?

AIDS puts forth an incredible "alphabet soup" of acronyms and terms to contend with.

"HIV" Terms

First, what is HIV? *HIV* stands for Human Immunodeficiency Virus. When someone has HIV in their blood system, they are said to be *infected with HIV*, or infected with the virus that causes AIDS.

An infected person is called *HIV-positive* only after taking a specific test that indicates whether their immune system has developed antibodies to fight off HIV or not. Developing antibodies and testing positive is also called *sero-conversion*. An uninfected person will normally test *HIV-negative* when taking this HIV antibody test.

An estimated 90 percent of all Americans infected with HIV do not yet know because they have not been tested. People who think they may be infected should get tested because then they have the opportunity to take certain treatments that can prolong their lives.

Being infected or HIV-positive is the first stage in *HIV disease*, which is the spectrum of stages leading from infection to full-blown AIDS. Often within weeks of infection, a person goes through an "acute infection" stage of severe flu-like symptoms—nausea, spiking fevers, night sweats, etc.—as the HIV multiplies rapidly and attacks the immune system.

After acute infection, people tend to have no major symptoms showing HIV is in their systems. This is called being *asymptomatic*. Currently, the asymptomatic stage lasts about seven to ten years. Then they will begin having serious health problems. Once symptoms start, their life-span *tends* to be radically shortened—unless God intervenes somehow, either through healing them or through medical research developments that slow the progress of HIV disease.

ARC—AIDS Related Complex

The second stage is called *ARC*, which stands for AIDS Related Complex. (Although this term has become obsolete, you still read it or hear it. A newer term for the same stage is *symptomatic HIV disease*.) In ARC, there are some physical manifestations of HIV disease. Primarily, these are night sweats and HIV wasting, which means rapid loss of weight from diarrhea and fevers brought on by HIV's deterioration of the immune system. Remember Dennis in chapter 11? He experienced radical weight loss of about thirty pounds in two weeks from HIV wasting. But he did not yet have any of the typical cancers, pneumonias, and infections that go with AIDS. So ARC is sort of halfway between being asymptomatic and having AIDS.

Full-Blown AIDS

The third stage is called *full-blown AIDS*: Acquired Immunodeficiency Syndrome. At this point, people begin contracting exotic infections that those with a normal, healthy immune system would never catch. These unusual, *opportunistic infections* are caused by fungi, bacteria, parasites, and viruses found all around us—in the air, on our clothes, in our bodies—everywhere. No one catches these infections unless their immune system is so depleted that their body cannot fight them off any longer. For instance, one friend of mine has permanent athlete's foot. He cannot get rid of it, no matter what spray he uses or how often he uses it; the athlete's foot just does not go away.

At the epidemic's beginning, researchers estimated that 10 percent of those infected would eventually contract full-blown AIDS. That estimate gradually increased. Now the general consensus seems to be that 100 percent of those infected will develop full-blown AIDS unless something intervenes.

Action Point 1. Coming to Terms with Terms

Importance of terms changes. As of January 1992, the official definition of AIDS changed to having a T-cell count under two hundred, which indicates the immune system is severely depleted. But the other terms are still quite useful.

Because symptoms may not begin showing up for ten full years, the AIDS epidemic of a decade from now is being set in cement today this hour, this minute. That is frightening. It means we have a solemn responsibility to do all we can to educate people about this disease, how it is transmitted, and how to prevent becoming infected.

As a side note, the term *AIDS victim* is considered derogatory or demeaning. *AIDS patient* is not so good either, because it connotes a person passively receiving treatment. We need to be aware that if we use these terms in talking to or about people with HIV disease, we may unwittingly insult someone and create barriers to the gospel for them. "Let your speech be always with grace," states Colossians 4:6, "seasoned with salt, that ye may know how ye ought to answer every man."

It seems the current consensus is to use *person with AIDS*, or, even better, *person living with HIV disease*. These stress the individual and not the disease. Or you do not refer to them by connecting them with their disease.

2. How Does HIV Disease Progress?

If you saw the film *Jurassic Park*, you will probably be able to pick up the basic concept of how HIV functions easier than you think. Early in the film everyone is shown a short cartoon about "Mr. DNA" that showed the recovery of dinosaur blood from insects stuck in amber. Then the Jurassic Park scientists extracted DNA from the blood. To fill any missing genes, they spliced in frog DNA, thinking these "neutral" genes would cause no harm. Also, they genetically programmed things so only female dinosaurs would be hatched. That would prevent unauthorized reproduction.

Attack from Within

But something went wrong. The dinosaur expert who took care of the two children stumbled across the remains of some hatched eggs. The frog gene splices transmogrified the dinosaur DNA and allowed the unanticipated creation of male dinosaurs, because certain frogs are able to change gender in the absence of the opposite gender.

Just as the frog DNA overpowered the dinosaur genes, HIV hides itself inside human T-cells in the blood, splices its genetic material into the human DNA, and then overpowers it—transforming the T-cells into tiny factories to produce strings and strings of new HIV genes. Then the new little HIV viruses burst out of their hijacked factory and create all kinds of havoc by infecting other T-cells and repeating the whole cycle.

Unfortunately, the T-cells are the very immune system cells that should attack HIV and kill it before it does the body any harm. So HIV has disarmed the immune system's response mechanism.

Eventually, an infected person's supply of T-cells becomes depleted as the HIV invade, replicate inside, and then kill the T-cell by bursting out. Since T-cells fight off diseases, the lower the T-cell count, the lower the resistance and the more likely a person is to catch diseases that he or she normally would not. And it is these *other* diseases—opportunistic infections—that kill. The only exception is if HIV gets into the nervous system. This leads to lesions on the brain, which results in dementia. Dementia is somewhat similar to Alzheimer's disease; people lose their thinking abilities, and often exhibit bizarre emotional responses to events.

Action Point 2. Treatment and Research

As you can glimpse by the devious way HIV works, finding treatments to stop HIV directly may be difficult. We need to pray for those working toward medical treatments, both to attack HIV directly and to attack the various opportunistic infections that later overtake the body, depleted of its defenses. We can also consider donating funds to reputable research foundations working on these problems. Additionally, we can pray for those we know that are HIV-infected, that their T-cell counts would stay high and that God would strengthen them physically to ward off opportunistic infections.

3. What Does the "HIV" Test Indicate?

The test we normally hear about, the ELISA test, does not test directly for HIV itself. Instead, it detects whether a person's immune system has responded to the presence of the foreign invader by creating antibodies. (*Antibodies* are proteins the body manufactures to neutralize any microbes that invade it.) Several more complex and expensive tests, like the Western blot test, actually detect the presence of HIV itself. The P24 antigen test detects whether HIV is dormant, based on particulates commonly found when HIV is active.

Action Point 3. Test-time Helpers

Getting an HIV antibody test can be a frightening experience for people who think they may be infected. Even though most cities offer anonymous test sites where a person does not have to disclose a real name, just the knowledge of possible infection can be devastating. Also, the usual ten-day to two-week period while awaiting the results can prove agonizing. Here, Christians can step in to act as a friend and prayer partner for those awaiting news of the test, and can pray for those who need to be tested but are reluctant. Also, you can consider driving your friends to the test site to pick up the results with them. They may be in shock, regardless of whether they test positive or negative, and should not be driving. Also, you may need to listen, console, encourage them, or rejoice—whatever the results require.

4. What Are the Modes of HIV Transmission?

Concerns directly related to transmission of HIV probably top the list of questions that arise at most teachings on HIV/AIDS.

+ Am I at risk because of such-and-such behavior I used to do (or still do)?

+ What about my kids? Are they at risk at elementary school or even Sunday School if there's another kid there with AIDS?

+ I heard about a boy catching HIV when another kid bit him—is that true?

+ Can I get HIV from mosquitoes? French kissing? Airborne particles? Someone's cough?

+ Is the government telling us the truth about this disease?

The list grows long. People are usually more afraid than curious. It is important to acknowledge our fears, but it is also important to take the initiative to educate ourselves and then move forward through our fears to a Christ-dependent life.

My resource library on AIDS includes over three hundred volumes on theological, medical, treatment, historical, counseling, and biographical perspectives. They take up eight shelves of space, three feet wide each—some double-stacked. I have come to realize that you could create a full-time job just keeping up with new research studies and findings that are being published daily! And yet, there is solid evidence that HIV is transmitted very few ways.

Following is a summary of what I have found in my research reading. In presenting these facts, I will use frank language without being overly graphic. I realize that some of the facts are things we would rather not have to know. But if we intend to live in the real world and minister to people in all kinds of situations, we will be better off knowing now than to be shocked into not ministering later when a person we meet is dealing with HIV.

Body Fluids and HIV

These body fluids definitely contain significant levels of HIV:

+ Blood, including menstrual blood
+ Semen
+ Vaginal and cervical secretions
+ Organ tissues
+ Breast milk

Low levels of HIV are found in these fluids:

+ Urine
+ Saliva
+ Tears

There is still debate about how much HIV is necessary to cause infection, but it is clear that the higher the level of HIV in a fluid, the more likely infection from it will be.

Sexual Intercourse

HIV can be transmitted via sexual intercourse—either anal or vaginal and rarely through oral. It has been documented that the route of infection can go in any direction: male-to-female, female-to-male, male-to-male, and female-to-female.

In the USA, the main mode of transmission was originally through male homosexual activity. That is gradually changing and the greatest rate of increase for infection is occurring among the heterosexual population. In Africa, transmission is primarily through heterosexual activity.

Receptive anal intercourse (male-to-male and male-to-female) constitutes perhaps the most "efficient" mode of transmission outside direct injection of HIV-infected blood, because the rectum has many blood vessels and is easily torn during anal intercourse, allowing infected semen direct access into the bloodstream.

Vaginal intercourse (male-to-female and female-to-male). This is less efficient than anal intercourse, but it can be made more dangerous by the presence of lesions (in either the male or female) caused by other sexually transmitted diseases, and—in some women—by micro-tears in the uterus caused by an allergic reaction irritation from nonoxynol-9. (Nonoxynol-9 is a spermicide used in conjunction with some condoms.)

Receptive oral sexual activity (male-to-male, female-to-female, male-to-female, and female-to-male). These are all rare forms of transmission, but there are documented cases of all four categories.

Some women have been infected via artificial insemination from infected semen, but sperm banks now routinely test for HIV.

Infected Needles or Equipment

HIV can be transmitted by using and/or sharing unsterilized hypodermic needles and equipment that are contaminated by infected blood in or on them.

In this category, the most obvious type of needle use would be intravenous drug users, for example, heroin users. But it goes beyond that to such activities as young people "shooting" steroids and other body-building concoctions.

Also, healthcare workers who sustain needle sticks in the course of their work with infected patients are at risk. According to one statistic, only .05 percent of all accidental needle sticks resulted in HIV infection. (That translates to one per two thousand sticks.)

Unsterilized dental equipment may have been the means of transmission in the Florida case where six patients of one dentist were infected. (In June of 1992, a friend of Dr. Acer who died of AIDS, stated that he concluded the dentist purposely infected those patients, believing that America would not take notice of the HIV epidemic until the old and the young were struck down with it.)

Although it is not known definitely if or how Dr. Acer may have infected these six patients, disinfection procedures at dental offices definitely have changed dramatically since the early 1990s. Disposable masks, gloves, and implements are the norm, as is sterilization of non-disposable tools and equipment.

Exposure to Blood and Organ Tissues

HIV can be transmitted via blood transfusions, infected blood by-products, and organ transplants.

Most people are aware of Ryan White, a hemophiliac who died of HIV disease. And they may recall the tragic account of hundreds of Romanian babies getting infected from injections of small amounts of tainted blood shortly after birth.

Direct exposure to significant amounts of infected blood is considered the most dangerous, "effective" means of acquiring HIV disease. Organ tissues and transplants are included in this category, since they contain blood. Also at risk are hemophiliacs (primarily males) infected via the blood clotting factor shots they took, which was isolated from the blood of over hundreds of donors. Since the mid-1980s, these blood products have been heat-treated to kill HIV.

Infection by transfusions of blood or blood products and organ transplants are now quite rare since the development of the HIV antibody test in 1985, which has made screening of infected blood and tissues easier. The current risk estimate of HIV infection from a blood transfusion is between 1 in 50,000 to 1 in 125,000. This risk occurs because there is a "window" of time in which a person's immune system responds with antibodies to HIV. Most people *sero-convert* (test positive for antibodies to HIV) within three months of infection and fully 99 percent sero-convert within six months. Also, the HIV antibody test gives a very rare "false nega-tive," meaning that infected blood with HIV antibodies tests nega-tive for their presence.

Healthcare providers may also be at risk of direct exposure to infected blood. For example, blood splashes onto mucous mem-branes (eye, nose, mouth) may occur. Or blood may contact their non-intact skin, with openings caused by dry, chapped, fissured, or inflamed skin; and conditions like dermatitis and severe acne.

Mother to Child and Vice Versa

HIV has rarely been transmitted between mother and child. This can occur in several ways, usually around the time of birth, also called *perinatally*. It may occur from mother to child in the womb, crossing the placenta. (HIV can be detected/cultured from the unborn child's tissue, amniotic fluid, placental tissues, and umbilical cord blood.)

Transmission of HIV can also occur during the birth process, by exposure to infected maternal blood. For example, one report of sixty-six sets of twins born to HIV-infected mothers, mostly from the USA, showed that the second-born twins more commonly were HIV-negative than first-born twins, whether the delivery method was vaginal or Cesarean. The first-born twin is exposed to more maternal blood during delivery than is the second-born twin.

Rarely, transmission may occur through milk while nursing. For example, there are at least twenty documented cases worldwide where mothers became HIV-infected after the child's birth and transmitted the virus during the acute infection stage, where HIV multiplies rapidly and the immune system cannot mount a suffi-cient response to stop it.

In extremely rare cases, transmission can occur after birth, but in reverse, with the infant infecting its mother. There were seven cases in Russia where infants were infected by unsterilized syringe needles at the hospital where they were born. Their fathers all were HIV-negative. Their mothers all became HIV-positive without any known or admitted risk factors other than their HIV-infected baby. All seven of these mothers had severe nipple cracks with bleeding, and their breastfed infants had severe ulcerations with bleeding in their mouths. Another ninety-four non-breastfeeding mothers were all HIV-negative, even with HIV-positive infants. (Apparently this was detected in the follow-up research on 152 cases of HIV infection of infants via unsterile syringe needles in Elista, Russia.)

Some people are aware that infants born to infected mothers initially test HIV-positive, but that this condition flip-flops to HIV-negative sometime later. There is an solid explanation for this apparent mystery. A baby does not have a strong immune system. For the first months, most of a child's protection against diseases comes through antibodies from the mother's milk. That is why a baby may test HIV-positive initially, if the mother is infected. But those HIV antibodies eventually go out of the baby's system, and the child later tests HIV-negative. Current statistics show that about 25 percent to 30 percent of babies born to HIV-infected mothers are themselves actually infected with the virus.

Casual Transmission and Other Modes of Infection

People commonly ask about casual transmission and apparently very exotic cases of someone contracting HIV. To quote *The Essential AIDS Fact Book,* 1991 edition:

> Many studies have been done on transmission patterns within the families of those with HIV infection and AIDS. No family member or housemate has contracted HIV infection from a person with AIDS other than sexual partners and children born to infected mothers. These people lived together without special precautions, sharing beds, dishes, clothing, toilets, food, toothbrushes, toys, and baby bottles.[2]

If HIV is transmitted through casual contact, why have *no* infections been linked to hugging, shaking hands, and other such casual contacts with infected individuals? In fact, it seems that fear about AIDS is more contagious than the virus itself. The *New Republic* magazine in 1985 coined the term AFRAIDS—Acute Fear Regarding AIDS—to express this other problem. This should challenge people to get beyond their fears, not to ridicule people who have legitimate questions about HIV disease. (And when the possible outcome is death, it is better to ask all questions than not!)

Other strong evidence exists against casual contagion:

+ There is an uneven gender distribution of AIDS—currently about 90 percent men and 10 percent women in the USA. If HIV were transmitted by airborne or casual contact means, you would expect the distribution to be fifty-fifty for men and women.

+ There is a skewed age distribution of AIDS throughout the world—mostly involving people in their twenties to forties. If HIV were transmitted through casual contact or airborne routes, you should expect to see closer to an even distribution by gender and by age.

+ Ongoing household and family member studies, even since the 1991 summary given above, show *no* transmission taking place from infected to uninfected members, except for sexual partners of the infected person, or someone who used a blood-contaminated instrument, such as a razor.

Here are some other specific concerns often voiced.

Saliva and Deep "French Kissing." Saliva may pose some danger of contagion, as it contains small amounts of blood, which would include infected white blood cells. It also contains small amounts of HIV, though HIV in saliva is not found in all people with HIV disease. There is increased risk of transmission in the presence of gingivitis (gum infection), bleeding gums, oral Herpes lesions, or canker sores—anything that gives HIV access to a person's bloodstream.

One commonly cited case is of an older couple where the husband reportedly infected his wife through kissing (that was the extent of their intimate involvement). But researchers apparently were not able to culture HIV repeatedly from her. So that case is inconclusive.

In my thinking, the real issue is not saliva and French kissing; it is the fact that if there is deep kissing going on between two individuals—especially two who are not married—it is unlikely they will stop there. Their passion is taking them dangerously close to going beyond reasonable boundaries, and they may end up engaging in sexual intercourse, which is very dangerous in terms of potential for infection taking place.

Some people misleadingly make light of the problem of saliva. For instance, one medical worker stated that because the concentration of HIV in saliva is so low, it would take about a quart of saliva to have enough HIV to cause possible infection through French kissing. A friend of mine involved with AIDS ministry shared this supposedly authoritative piece of information during a presentation to a group of teenagers. One girl immediately raised her hand and asked, "Is that all at once, or over the course of a year?" Although it may well be true that saliva does not contain much HIV, there is reasonable room for caution without becoming phobic about exposure to minute quantities of saliva.

Bites. At least two cases of transmission of HIV, apparently by bites, have been reported. One involved a woman with HIV who got in a fight, had broken teeth and bleeding in her mouth, and deeply bit another woman, who became infected. That case seems pretty clear. The second does not: It involved two young hemophiliac brothers—one infected and the other not. Their mother recalls seeing a bruise mark on the uninfected son's arm, apparently from his brother biting him—but the skin was not broken. He later became infected. This case is unclear as to transmission because there may have been other modes of transmission open, such as accidental mixing of the hypodermic needle equipment for shots of clotting factor.

During the same time period when these cases of possible transmission were reported, there were also *numerous* documented reports (over sixty cases) where healthcare workers were bitten—some severely—by AIDS patients who had dementia. Not one of these healthcare workers sero-converted, even after follow-up tests (which are usually administered another six months later). I believe that confirms the basic conclusion: HIV is not casually transmitted.

Other Body Fluids and By-Products. There is a plausibility of infection through urine, tears, vomit, and feces, although this is unlikely. Although their concentrations of HIV may be exceedingly small or almost nil, they may carry hidden blood, which is potentially dangerous. Still, healthcare workers, who are perhaps the most likely to be exposed to these, are warned to take precautions such as wearing latex gloves and using a bleach solution when cleaning up vomit.

Transmission by Mosquitoes. Both general evidence (such as that against casual contagion) and specific evidence exists that contradicts the idea of mosquitoes passing HIV.

✦ No replication of HIV in mosquito or other insect cell lines has been detected in laboratory studies. In other words, the HIV fed to the mosquitoes and other insects died; it did not divide.

✦ In one study, mosquitoes were allowed to feed on HIV-infected blood samples. Then they were shaken off and given uninfected blood to feed on. Later, the second batch of blood was tested to see if it had been infected by blood from the mosquitoes. The second sample proved free of HIV.

✦ There is an uneven gender distribution and skewed age distribution of HIV disease, but mosquitoes are "equal opportunity biters." If HIV were transmitted by mosquitoes, you would expect a fifty-fifty ratio for men and women and an equal percentage of people in all age categories to be infected.

This is my conclusion: There are things of which to be cautious—especially exposure to blood—but it is very improbable you would become infected simply by casual social contact with someone with HIV disease. The problem lies more in our attitudes and fears than anything else.

Action Point 4. Education and Prevention Support

The issue of HIV transmission raises all kinds of emotions in people: fear, doubt, anger, frustration. We can pray that Christians who are accurately informed on these issues will have opportunities to educate others about ways HIV infection can occur and how to prevent that. We can also pray that people change behaviors that put them at risk, and that our churches will offer support programs for people who want to change risk behaviors that are addictions.

5. How Do You Prevent Infection?

Someone with full-blown AIDS is absolutely more likely to catch some sort of illness from you than you are of contracting HIV disease from them in a social or work setting. Still, there is one basic rule to remember in all situations, whether you have casual contact with a person with AIDS, you live with him or her, or you are a healthcare worker: *Avoid direct exposure to blood or body fluids.*

Here are some examples of the application for this rule.

+ In cleaning up any kind of spills that may have blood in them (including vomit, feces, etc.) or other body fluids, avoid direct exposure. This applies even if your skin appears intact (has no cuts or abrasions). Use rubber or latex gloves. Apply a disinfecting bleach solution of one part bleach to nine parts water. Flush paper towels down the toilet or dispose of in a sealed plastic bag.

+ Do not share personal items that have hidden blood or body fluids on them, such as dental equipment (toothbrushes, toothpicks, denture cups); shaving equipment of any kind; personal grooming equipment (tweezers, nail clippers or scissors, etc.); makeup; pierced earrings. All of these may carry minute amounts of blood from micro-cuts in the skin.

+ Do not share eating utensils or drinking vessels with each other at the same meal. (Seeing people share cups or forks always bothers me anyway!) There is no problem, though, if you re-use utensils a person with AIDS has used, once they have been adequately washed. Disposables are not necessary.

If you have regular contact with someone with HIV, there are other specific things you should do to maintain a living environment that is safe and healthy for both yourself and the other person. An excellent book with practical recommendations that are both easy to understand and easy to implement is *AIDS Care at Home*.[3] (See bibliography for details.)

Is "Safe" Sex Really Safe?

No, it is not. Even many organizations that promoted "safe" sex early on in this epidemic now promote *"safer"* sex. They recognize that condom usage is not one hundred percent safe, or perhaps they simply do not want to take civil liability for giving the impression that it is 100 percent safe. The only truly "safe" sex is abstinence—forgoing sexual intimacy until marriage—and then remaining mutually faithful sexually within marriage.

Safe-sex campaigns generally do not acknowledge the truth that condoms fail at times, both because of the condom itself being faulty and because it may be used incorrectly. Tests have shown that condoms fail to prevent pregnancy about 16 percent of the time. Many have made the analogy of this being like playing "Russian roulette," with one bullet in a six-chamber handgun.

If there is one issue perhaps more than any other related to HIV that has agitated theologically conservative Christians, it is the whole concept of "safe" sex. This concept-turned-program has been used to justify the introduction of comprehensive sex education into schools and to endorse homosexuality as the moral equivalent of heterosexuality. Perhaps most outrageous of all, it seems to assume that people (especially teenagers) have no self-control and will engage in sex regardless, so you might as well tell them to "protect" themselves.

Teenagers have lately been disproving the assumption that they have no self-control. True Love Waits is an international campaign designed to challenge teenagers and college students to remain sexually pure until marriage. Hundreds of thousands of young people have signed covenant cards making a commitment "to be sexually abstinent from this day until the day I enter a biblical relationship." In July 1994 more than 210,000 covenant cards were displayed on the National Mall in Washington, D.C.

Action Point 5. Hospitality, Truth, and Support

As Christians, we should lead the way by our willingness to be hospitable to those who have AIDS. We should make the slight personal accommodations necessary to make them feel more comfortable and safe around us. We can be supportive of people unreasonably afraid of HIV and those infected and seek gently to point them to the truths that their risk of infection is tiny and that true love casts out fear (see 1 John 4:18).

And we should also be willing to speak the truth in love about remaining sexually pure until marriage, the significant lack of safety in so-called "safe sex," and God's forgiveness for those who have broken His commandments about engaging in sex outside of marriage.

But telling the truth is not enough. We need to support through prayer and finances, and perhaps volunteering, those Christians who teach an abstinence-based message and counsel those who have slipped, as well as those who desire to change if they have become sexually addicted.

Being a Berean

This chapter has presented essential facts about medical and transmission issues related to HIV. But you need to be convinced of them for yourselves. If the Lord brings people with AIDS into your life, it will not be enough for you that I believe HIV is not casually transmitted. You may have doubts and worries about whether you will catch HIV, and people with AIDS will pick up on your uncertainty. Not being fully convinced for yourselves may block potential avenues of ministry or developing relationships with people who are HIV-positive.

Romans 14:22–23 states that whatever is not of faith is sin. In that context, Christians took actions based on the strength of conviction someone else had on certain questions. Then they had doubts and felt condemned, guilty. So it caused them to stumble, because they took action before they were sure in their own minds about what they should be doing.

Scripture gives us a solution for this problem in Acts 17: "And the brethren . . . sent away Paul and Silas by night into Berea; who coming thither, went into the synagogue of the Jews. These [the Bereans] were more noble than those in Thessalonica, in that they received the word with all readiness of mind, and searched the scriptures daily, whether those things were so. Therefore, many of them believed"(vv. 10–12a).

They checked it out for themselves. We cannot live on someone else's faith—not in the Christian walk, not in AIDS ministry.

A wise piece of advice a friend gave me is this: Your decision is only as good as your information. So I strongly urge you to get *The AIDS Epidemic: Balancing Compassion and Justice* by Glenn Wood and John Dietrich—both medical doctors. I suggest you read chapters 6 through 9 on the medical description of AIDS. Work through any doubts and fears you have, so you do not feel condemned or anxious when you interact with people affected by HIV. Have a conviction about transmission—not just an opinion.

If you are looking for an excuse to avoid people with AIDS—or any other kind of problem—you will always be able to find one. Regardless, Scripture admonishes us that true love casts out fear.

PART FOUR

Reaping the Harvest

CHAPTER THIRTEEN

The Fields Are Ready: The Battle between the Kingdom and the World

THE NOISE OF THE HIGHWAY AROUND ME INTENSIFIED AS I PUT ON my turn signal and slowed down. A huge semi-truck lumbered toward me. Crossing traffic, I turned onto the dirt road. Then, bumping over the cattle guard, I drove along the lane past the head-high grapevines.

Since grapes are a major source of farm revenues for California, we take them seriously. The vines along the dirt road leading to the stable were well tended and obviously productive. Pickers had been there two days before to remove most of the grapes and pile the fruit high onto waiting trucks. Now the denuded vines looked vacant, save a cluster here and there hanging on as if waiting to be remembered.

Suddenly, above me a flock of starlings wheeled around and swooped down into the vines. I held my breath and watched in awe as the birds dove past my car to fly through the vineyard. Right in front of my eyes, one bird slowed almost imperceptibly and raked at a cluster of grapes as it sped past. The shaking, broken cluster bled drops of juice. Some of the grapes fell to the ground and rolled away in the dust. Unbidden the words came to mind: *These were left after the harvest. They were not picked. They were unwanted.*

As I had prayed about this book one morning during praise and worship in church, I remembered clearly the men who had stood in front of us on Love In Action Night. *Look at them,* I heard God say. *The sixteen men you saw are part of the harvest of the last days. But for many churches, they are an unwanted harvest. They are overlooked by the reapers.*

Jesus warned his disciples of this very thing: "Say not ye, There are yet four months, and then cometh harvest? behold, I say unto you, Lift up your eyes, and look on the fields; for they are white already to harvest" (John 4:35).

Have we decided how and when the harvest will come? Jesus says, "Open your eyes and look out there. The harvest is at hand! Reap it!"

Fight for the Harvest

Today, one group of people remains largely untargeted by our churches for evangelism and redemptive ministry: the gay and lesbian community. Every day we see its members—at the grocery store, the post office, at work, in church.

Why are we not trying to reach them? And worse, why do we often turn them away when they begin to ask the tough questions:

+ If I get saved, will I have to leave my lover?
+ If I'm HIV-positive, will God protect me from AIDS after I turn my life over to Him?
+ Will there be a "safe" member of my own sex in the church who'll spend time with me and help me learn how to be a man/woman?

Where can they go? Is this group doomed to be as the grapes left on the vine? The devil will surely come in, as the starlings did, and slash at them as they wait. What can we do about it?

George, a man in his early thirties, had been involved in homosexual activities for years; in fact, he was sexually addicted. He heard of Love In Action and thought it might have the help he needed. But he almost did not get a chance, even though he had been accepted to the live-in program!

Realizing that a promising young man was about to get away, the gay community pulled out all the stops to try to draw him back into the lifestyle. His former lover notified a heterosexual woman known for her endorsement and support of those pursuing a "gay Christian" life. She flew hundreds of miles at her own expense, specifically to dissuade George from following through and moving to Love In Action. Fortunately, his resolve was stronger than her pro-gay propaganda.

Why didn't they just let George pursue the non-gay Christian life that he so desperately wanted? The gay activist communities know how to exploit weaknesses, confusion, and doubts. And they know the value of recruiting. They know that the interest they show in a man or woman can pay off. They are very aggressive in their efforts!

Working in our schools, governments, social services, and churches, their gay agendas are moving forward like the wheeling flock of starlings through the forgotten grapes. Here are just a few examples of society-wide actions that carry spiritual implications.

Schools

Project 10 began in a Los Angeles area school district as an informal program supposedly helping counsel high school students who thought they might be homosexual. It eventually transformed into a formal, gay-affirmative program that presumes young people confused about their sexuality are actually homosexual or bisexual and generally affirms them in experimenting to find out.

Besides adopting programs similar to Project 10, many districts are incorporating comprehensive sex education curricula that present homosexuality as a natural, normal variant of sexual orientation.

Government

A battle rages over so-called "gay rights." Although proponents strongly assert that the rights they seek are the same as for any other group, opponents are equally strong in their assertion that these constitute special rights, granted on a behavior-based lifestyle rather than an unchangeable condition like race or ethnic background.

Part of the problem stems from what may be *some* legitimate claims. For instance, in general, people should not be discriminated against in their job because of who they are or what they do on their own time. But if we happen to accept this premise, does that also mean that gays should have *all* the same rights and opportunities, such as to enjoy the legal and financial benefits that married couples do, to become foster parents, or to adopt children? No.

Social Services

Perhaps the most obvious example of the gay community taking social service leadership is in providing help to people with HIV/AIDS. As one formerly gay man with AIDS stated with great disappointment, "I can go to my church to find help for my soul and spirit. But I have to go back to the gay community to find help for my body, because the church doesn't want to get into that area."

Another tells how local gay AIDS organizations gave food, funds to pay utility bills, and even rent when he could no longer work to provide for himself. "My church had other priorities. I went where I could get help," he said.

Churches

All major denominations—Catholic, Protestant, Orthodox, Pentecostal, Charismatic, and evangelical—have pro-gay contingents and organizations, even though these are not necessarily given official sanction. A recent newsletter article from one particular denomination's pro-gay group instructed gay church members on how to go about their work. They were to disrupt and in every way possible make life uncomfortable for other church goers. They were to enter every area of church life—the nursery, the choir, the leadership—and do anything to raise a fuss and keep things in turmoil. In this way, it would be easier to create a unity when peace was offered that met the gay community's preferences.

With such committed, concerted efforts, no wonder gays and lesbians find so much success for their agendas. They see the fields. They go out and reap. What are churches doing? What are you doing?

Whose Harvest Is It?

Let us assume we want our churches to be healing churches. How can that happen?

First, we need to realize that we are the servants; His is the harvest. This is God's work, and we are merely privileged to be allowed to assist on His project, sort of like midwives helping a mother birth her child. Even Jesus humbled Himself in this same attitude about redemption's work He undertook in dying on the cross: "Jesus saith unto them, My meat is to do the will of him that sent me, and to finish his work. . . . And he that reapeth receiveth wages, and gathereth fruit unto life eternal: that both he that soweth and he that reapeth may rejoice together. And herein is that saying true, one soweth, and another reapeth. I sent you to reap that whereon ye bestowed no labour: other men laboured, and ye are entered into their labours" (John 4:34, 36–38).

Jesus wants us to understand that the harvest we look for belongs to God. We do not own the field. We have not done all the work. We are merely laborers who do not even know when the harvest is meant to be gathered. But those who receive instruction from Him who owns the field and who gather at His Word will be well paid in the fruit of life eternal and will rejoice with the other sowers and reapers.

As workers, it is humbling to realize we are not in charge of what God does. When we give our lives and resources to the work, sometimes we think we own a piece of the field. In reality, we own nothing—not even ourselves. We are simply field hands who work at the bidding of a gracious Master who employed us after saving our ruined lives.

A great harvest exists, but it is God's harvest. He is not trying to build our churches or advance our programs. His own plan is to bring people to salvation in Jesus Christ. He knows better than we do where they have been. And frankly, He is more concerned with where they go.

What about us? Why do we oppose homosexuality? Are we concerned with the poverty of spirit it causes others? Or are we worried about ways it affects our own comforts? *Homosexuality is an uncomfortable issue for everyone.* But the worst thing is not the problems it causes society as a whole, but the terrible destruction it ravages on the world—one man and woman at a time. This disaster can best be addressed by one person helping another person. In fact, one state's political coalition to stop the progress of gay rights has also begun a ministry wing called HOPE: Help One Person Escape.

The Battlefield

In the Christian community today, many believers feel embattled. The Bible says that our battle is not with flesh and blood. And yet, so often, we make war against flesh and blood.

Why are we fighting? We say it is to protect our freedom to express our faith. But do we really need anyone else's approval for that? Paul did it in prison and thereby led others to God.

To what battle has God called us? What is our service in Him? Has He not called us to set oppressed men and women free? They may not choose to respond, because freedom from this world's bondages means service to the Lord Jesus Christ. But if they do turn to God, are we there to help them along the way toward entering into all He intends? Do we ask God to protect us from the effects of the gay agenda, or are we really trying to advocate for those who may be caught up in the sin of homosexuality?

Make no mistake, a gay agenda seeks to legitimize homosexuality and to favor politically gay men, lesbians, bisexuals, and the behaviors they endorse. Are we Christians merely responding to a political threat, or have we been zealously caught up with God's all-powerful Holy Spirit in a majestic battle to win back those lost in sin?

Understand me: I do not oppose the fight that many evangelicals wage against the darkness in the gay community. But I do wonder at our purpose in the fight. What is our perspective? What do we want to achieve? Have we asked God what He wants us to achieve?

I believe in standing against our society's lawless element. It poses as a peacemaker, but it wants a peace that nods to immorality and winks at sin. As Christ's followers, we know well the source of the strength for this worldly political machine. But we must also realize that though we hold the line against immorality in the name of political action, we can still extend God's love and the hope of salvation in Jesus Christ. What other hope is there? Who will offer it if we fail?

What Harvest Do We Seek?

Peter, a man in his twenties, attended the same church for many years. He was not yet a Christian, though he had "tried" to be one. He simply never gave his life to Jesus. And there was a lot in his life he did not think Jesus would want. "In grade school, the other kids always made fun of me. I had a high voice and was overweight. They'd call me 'Fatso.' When I got to high school 'Fatso' turned to 'Faggot,'" he told me.

"What happened in your church?" I wondered aloud.

"By the time I got to church, I'd had several awful experiences with supposed Christians that shook my faith in other men. One peer counselor seduced me. A pastor gave me pro-gay literature. Another counselor administered a sexuality test and told me flatly, 'Not much hope, is there?' I finally became afraid of getting into a trust situation with any man who could speak into my life. I'd think, 'It's going to happen again.'"

"What did happen?" I asked.

"Well, I did get saved. But when I went to the pastor and told him about my struggles, he didn't treat them as a 'real' problem. I wasn't the first homosexual to darken their door. But they didn't have a plan to deal with the needs involved in ministry to gays or lesbians."

"Why not?" I asked incredulously.

"They don't think the problem exists—and the pastor runs the show!"

"What do you mean?"

"They aren't looking at the needs that come to them. The pastor makes a decision about what they'll do and that's what they go with."

Peter got the help he needed at Love In Action. But the healing process will take many years as he slowly learns that just because some of God's servants are not interested in Peter's problem does not mean that He is not interested.

Do you remember the story of David being chosen king over Israel? God sent the prophet Samuel to the town of Bethlehem where he called Jesse and his sons to come with him to sacrifice before the Lord. As each of Jesse's sons passed before him, Samuel spoke with God regarding which he was to choose as king. Each time Samuel thought he had found God's man, the Lord corrected him: "But the LORD said unto Samuel, Look not on his countenance, or on the height of his stature; because I have refused him: for the LORD seeth not as man seeth; for man looketh on the outward appearance, but the LORD looketh on the heart" (1 Sam. 16:7).

Sadly, this is all too true. Many churches are like pickers in the vineyard. Some people are attractive. Maybe they are easier to reach. Whatever our reasons, we pick them and overlook others. What happens to those who are overlooked? Like the leftover clusters of grapes, they are often at the mercy of destructive forces from this world.

But if we are workers in the Lord's fields, then we are called to harvest men's and women's lives: To secure their souls from eternal destruction and, having done so, to encourage their continued walk into wholeness and completion in Christ.

What is the *wanted* harvest? Would we not all prefer to pick the fat clusters off the vine at their peak of ripeness? And the grain?

Who would not prefer to cut the full heads of grain as they stand? Likewise, which of us would not like to usher men and women into God's kingdom who might at the same time elevate the status of our personal kingdom here? Why do we prefer one person over another when God sent His Son to die for all, equally? How much of our refusal to minister to people is simply that they do not meet our expectations? What do we expect? If we are honest, we much prefer well-adjusted, well-employed, healthy, and happy people. But Jesus came for the sick, the poor, the weak, and the downcast. We are called to carry on His work. As Jesus said: "They that are whole have no need of the physician, but they that are sick: I came not to call the righteous, but sinners to repentance" (Mark 2:17).

Where Are the Gleaners?

Later in the summer I came upon another example of the unwanted harvest. Along the same dirt road by the vineyards are hay fields. The summer wears on and the hay is cut. In time, the farmer comes out and burns the stubble of the field. Among the stubble however, lie many seeds dropped as the hay is cut. But the hay farmer is not concerned with these gleanings, for it is not cost-effective to try to glean the oats from a hay field. So thick smoke rises in a choking tribute to the death of all as fire consumes what is left behind.

In Israel's fields, harvesters left gleanings for the poor. Ruth and Naomi lived from gleaning the fields of their kinsman, Boaz. This was God's provision, as the Lord commanded through Moses: "[W]hen ye reap the harvest of your land, thou shalt not wholly reap the corners of thy field, neither shall thou gather the gleanings of thy harvest. And thou shalt not glean thy vineyard, neither shalt thou gather every grape of thy vineyard; thou shalt leave them for the poor and stranger: I am the LORD your God" (Lev. 19:9–10).

How hard to pick up grain, kernel by kernel by kernel, until there is enough for a meal. And yet, how valuable the gleaned grain is to those truly hungry! It is difficult to harvest; yet, once gathered, it is every bit as useful for food as the first grain which drops on the threshing floor.

Trevor, part of Love In Action's live-in program, has been in our church for two years. He ran with my daughter Becky in the three-legged race at this year's Mother's Day picnic. They fell halfway through the race and laughed so hard they could not stand up. So he simply held her and crawled on. Later, he sat by me and shared a part of his mom's story.

"The Lord gave me a perfect opportunity to tell my mother I was infected with HIV," he said. "We were at the Exodus Conference and neither of us had a class or anything. We were alone together. 'Mom,' I said. 'I have something to tell you. I'm HIV-positive.'"

"How did she respond?"

"She burst into tears and cried for a few minutes. I tried to stop her. 'Don't cry,' I said. 'I don't have AIDS yet.' I felt so bad to see how much I'd hurt her.

"Then she scolded me. 'Don't tell me to stop crying. I have a right to grieve! Allow me that,' she said. Then she sort of pulled herself up and we went on with the conversation."

"Your mother sounds pretty neat," I smiled.

" That she is. She talks to me about it every once in a while. 'You would tell me if something was wrong, wouldn't you?' she'll ask me. I always reassure her that, yes, I would let her know."

"How are you doing with it? Trevor, how do you live knowing you have the virus that causes AIDS?" I asked.

"I live with purpose. I want my life to count for God," he answered. "I want to help others avoid the mistakes I made."

Every time I talk to someone like Trevor, I thank God for hungry gleaners who search the fields for every kernel. I know many more like this man could be reached if more of God's workers engaged in God's business rather than their own.

In Harvest Time

As I began writing this book, my husband and I went one day to Sebastopol, a town somewhat north and light-years into the country near us. Each autumn, this community of small farms opens its pumpkin patches for jack-o-lanterns. The patch we found nestled in a small valley beside a quiet two-lane road was nonetheless a favorite stopping place for school buses full of children.

We had the whole day. So we found a bench, sat in the golden sunlight that is a part of autumn alone, and watched the laughing children run through the patch and pick out their pumpkins. How warm the sun was! A tiny breeze fluttered the poplar leaves above us. The startling blue skies above and brilliant orange pumpkins lying amongst the aging vines brought a sense of completion and peace.

The harvest is truly a beautiful thing! The promise of bounty lies in gilded and bright abundance before you. But as the cool nights and warm days of autumn give way to the cold and storms of post-harvest winter, what a stark and frightening contrast there is. The pumpkin patch in winter is a dead, forbidding place until the rotting, blackened corpses are plowed under.

Many Christians today believe that we are in the harvest time of the world. There is yet a window of opportunity in which to see gays and lesbians turn to God and away from sin. But we must pass through the fields now! While the harvest is at hand, we must reap. Soon will come the winter of this world. Though the saved will rejoice in that day of their redemption, the lost will be lost forever. While there is golden light in which to work, get out into the fields and reap!

———

Gathering the Harvest:
Accounts of Successful Reaping

THE CHEERY VOICE ON THE OTHER END OF THE PHONE LAUGHED when I asked, "Are you busy?"

"Oh, yes," Aunt Katie said. "It's that time of year. But we're having so much fun, too. Yesterday I was watching one of the grandsons and we were out in the garden working when the neighbor's truck pulled up. Seems he was taking donuts to the men in the orchards and thought we needed some refreshment. 'Pick yourself out a donut,' he said. My little grandson picked the big chocolate one, of course." Here she laughed again—a bright musical sound.

"It sounds so wonderful, but I've been hearing how hot it is, too."

"It's always hot! You know, I think it's just a shame the harvest doesn't come in the winter when it's cool," she chuckled. "Then you wouldn't mind spending so much time in front of a hot stove."

"What are you working on now?" I asked her.

"My tomatoes are coming in now. We trade a lot, too, though. Yesterday the neighbor lady brought me down a box of peaches. So I have lots to do."

I could imagine the scene. I knew the lady she mentioned, how she wore a bandana when working in the peaches. I had tasted her peaches, too, while sitting in Aunt Katie's kitchen and watching as she cut them into an oversized bowl. That room was a place where comfort invaded every corner like the smell of cinnamon from a baking pie. Just thinking about it made me homesick for the little town where Mike was born.

"Seems the last time I was up there at this time of year, the farmers were shaking the prune trees," I reminisced.

"They started that about two days ago," Aunt Katie agreed.

"That's a pretty dirty operation, isn't it?" I asked.

"Yeah, dirt, dirt, dirt. Everybody drives around with it on their cars and all. Even so, we all complain but no one really minds," she reflected.

"Why?" I asked.

"I can't really say. Big trucks keep rumbling by, the neighbors all drop in, and it's a friendly time—a happy time. We all have a big party at the end where everyone brings food. You get caught up with neighbors and everyone's glad for what they've accomplished."

There is no place on earth with the energy to rival a farming community in the harvest. As the long summer growing season winds down, the activity of bringing in the crop speeds up. Hard work has paid off, abundance is stored, and the reward of a job well done is enjoyed.

In ministry we experience times of harvest, too. Though they do not happen at a specific time of year, the growing seasons change and the "crop" is brought in. One life changed is worth many seasons of toil.

One day I took a walk with a woman named Dawn and talked about the harvest God was bringing in her life. Through her, I've learned some things about "harvesting" the lives of former gays and lesbians—elements needed in all of us if we desire to be successful at reaping for God.

Availability

The summer, drawing to an end, had grown progressively hotter. To stay cool, Dawn and I walked in the early evening. As we did, I quizzed her. "Tell me about this week coming up. I hear you have some big plans."

The young woman beside me chuckled. "God is opening doors in amazing ways!" she laughed. "This weekend Vivian and I go to a federal prison near here to share our testimonies. Then, on Monday, I'm going to Florida to formally apologize to the navy for burning down their building."

Dawn Killion's bright blue eyes twinkled in joy. This was her idea of fun! First spending a day in prison and then going to humbly ask forgiveness of a navy base commander? What kind of woman was she, anyway?

Most certainly a very different woman from the convicted felon of fifteen years before. Drunk, drugged, and outraged that the navy had discharged her friend because of lesbianism, Dawn threw a firebomb into a navy building. She had not intended to burn it down, but she did. While serving part of her seven-year prison sentence, she turned over her life to God.

"I was a very angry person. I felt completely unwanted and worthless. My appearance was hard and masculine—you know, cigarette pack in my front pocket and a comb in my back one." But she changed after meeting Christ.

Dawn was released in 1982 and began a rough and rocky pilgrimage that brought her to Love In Action and the Church of the Open Door in San Rafael where she has remained and grown. She now leads groups for women, counsels them, and prays for them. Whenever possible, she goes to prisons to help women there see that God can bring change.

"I've realized lately that I don't want people to identify me as the girl who burned down a navy building. That's one reason I decided to go to Jacksonville. I served a prison term but I never really apologized for what I did. Somehow I couldn't close that chapter and go on until I made the apology."

A counseling ministry based in Jacksonville, Florida, learned about Dawn's story at the 1994 Exodus Conference. Myra Noyes, the director, remembered the original incident and praying for the young woman who was convicted. Knowing now it was Dawn and seeing how much God had turned her life around, Myra felt Jacksonville should hear Dawn's story. She arranged the meeting with the base commander.

The following week, after Dawn came back home, she and I walked again and I heard about the meeting with the navy representative. "What happened?" I asked her. "Was he friendly or very austere?"

"I think he was worried at first it might be a publicity stunt. When he found out I was sincere, he was very gracious. 'I can't extend the navy's forgiveness,' he told me. 'But I can, on their behalf, receive your apology.' That's really all I was after."

Dawn was obedient to what she had been told to do: Go and apologize. Her faithful availability put her in a unique situation, carrying a precious message about God to people who might otherwise be insulated from it.

Sensitivity

Dawn and I walked on as the summer evening deepened. "Was that it? Or was there more to the meeting?" I asked.

"No. I mentioned that I'd understood that people had lost belongings in the fire. He said, 'Yes, and one of them is in this room.' I turned to the only other officer besides the chaplain and began to apologize. As I looked at him, I was struck with sorrow for the harm I'd done him. 'You lost things in the fire?' I asked. He nodded. 'I'm so sorry,' I said."

"Did you feel he accepted your apology?"

"Yes. I felt the sorrow so deeply, I think he could tell. I believe he really forgave me. I asked him, 'Were you at my trial?' and he said, 'Yes.' So it must have been pretty important to him."

God allowed the sorrow for what she had done to touch Dawn's heart, making her sensitive to the loss this man had suffered. It was not contrived and he knew it. God reached through her to touch him because she was sensitive and also because she was transparently honest.

Looking sidelong at the pretty, slight woman beside me, I marveled again at God's ability to transform. Her outward appearance had altered dramatically since her prison days. More importantly, her sense of God's love and her security in His love had changed her inside. Renewal was very real for Dawn. But how it must have impacted this man, who saw the before and after, I could only imagine. "Why do you think God is letting this all happen now?" I wondered aloud.

"I don't understand it, but I know His timing is perfect. If you'd told me a year ago I would be doing this, I wouldn't have believed it. Then I wasn't ready. Now I am."

Vulnerability: A Harvester's Secret

"Stepping into that room full of strangers must have been frightening," I noted.

"Yeah," she said, but reconsidered. "I was very nervous, but at the same time aware that God ushered me through. There was a rightness about it all—a comfort and a peace. I was just trying to catch up with what God was doing. It was like doors flew open and I was just walking through them."

"So, though you were in a vulnerable spot, you weren't afraid?"

She nodded in agreement. "It was strange, but I felt safe. Unusually safe. From the moment I took it to the Lord, I felt good about it."

Dawn's story reminded me of a past connection between vulnerability and the harvest. One year my boys, Jon and Jared, about four and six respectively, helped me plant carrots in our vegetable garden. I read about carrots, tried to prepare the soil well, planted according to directions, and tended the growing plants. My boys helped me and impatiently asked daily, "When can we eat the carrots?"

That summer our family vacation was very late, right about the time the carrots should have been harvested. We watered carefully the day after our return and then went out to pull our carrots up. Jon bit in first.

"It tastes like wood," he said, his face contorted in disgust. Since Jon had fallen and buried his top front teeth in the backyard retaining wall months before, we figured he knew what he was talking about! But Jared and I both tasted anyway.

"These are awful," Jared agreed.

It was unanimous. "They must have been in the ground too long," I sighed. "Sorry, kids." We washed the carrots and assembled the twenty-pound pile on the patio. We had grown carrots, but they were inedible because we had waited too long to harvest them.

As the Scripture states: "To every thing there is a season, and a time to every purpose under heaven" (Eccles. 3:1).

As there are appointed times for everything, in every harvest there is an element of vulnerability. An optimal time when reaping should begin balances against a susceptibility to disaster from various elements. An important part of gathering the harvest is knowing how and when to reap.

I have learned this for carrots and seen it apply to people. For instance, the pre-prison Dawn Killion would not have listened to the truth of God's love. But, in prison for a serious offense, she became ready. When the time was right, God sent a messenger and Dawn was saved.

Now, if no one had been there to bring the message, the window of opportunity might have passed for this young woman. Our responsibility is trusting by faith to the correct timing of things. God is the Master Farmer, we are field hands. We need His timing.

A farmer takes chances. If he plants too early and the rains come, his seed may be washed away. If he waits too long to harvest, counting on higher production, he may lose a good part of his crop. But if he fails to plant and reap for fear of the outcome, he will never have a harvest at all.

Dawn heard the call to go and apologize to the navy for her crime. She did not know any more, nor did she need to. The timing was right and God used the trip.

Reaping All That Is Sown

Perhaps one thing that makes us feel vulnerable is the certainty that everything which is sown will be reaped. Dawn's life was not easy once she turned it over to God. It would be so simple to look at her now and forget the difficulties she experienced. We cannot do that when we minister to people struggling with homosexuality and lesbianism.

Sins from the past, though forgiven, still have to be reckoned with. Because of her rebellion toward God, Dawn acted against the authority of people, too. The laws she broke resulted in time in prison.

But though we reap all that is sown, God can use it for His good purpose, making it worthwhile for us to endure. Through her time in prison, God taught this woman about real freedom in Jesus. "I thought at one point that I would die if I didn't get away from that barbed-wire fence," she told me. "That was about the time I sent in my second appeal for parole. I prayed and asked God to take a year off the forty-two months my sentence had already been reduced to. I wasn't saved yet, but He answered that prayer. Then I received Jesus as my Savior and everything changed."

"How? What was different?" I asked.

"Well, of course, I was different. Being in prison became a blessing. I learned the barbed wire was just a fence to protect me from myself and the world I couldn't deal with—I was cloistered. You see, before prison I'd entered into a criminal way of life. I couldn't keep a job and kept getting into trouble. During the year and a half I spent in prison after I got saved, God discipled and restored me. Then I was capable of going back into society and handling basic responsibilities."

Intrigued, I asked, "Dawn, what are you sowing now?"

"I'm trying to sow into other people's lives what I learned myself in prison—that there is hope and the possibility for change. I'm comforting others with the same comfort I've received. That's what the Lord told the Gaderene demoniac to do. I identify with that man from the tombs. So do others in prison and in lesbianism. My message to them is simple: Nobody is beyond Jesus' reach.

"When Vivian and I went to the prison two weeks ago, the trip's impact on my life astonished me. I saw how far God had brought me. I realized who I used to be. I thought 'I'm so different now, I wonder if they'll be able to relate to me or if I'll even relate to them?'"

"Did you have trouble?" I questioned, completely caught up in her story.

"Not once I got started. I felt empowered because I knew the truth! They could give their lives to Christ and really make a change. They didn't have to be stuck in the revolving door that prison becomes to so many. Lesbianism wasn't the main focus of what I said, but it was a point of showing them how to turn away from sin."

Adaptability

A few days later I took a walk with Vivian. She had made the trip to the women's prison in Southern California with Dawn. In a temperature of one hundred degrees—the prison inmates sat for an hour on blacktop pavement in the sun with no shade at all, just to hear the testimonies of these two young women. Why? Because they were bored? Not at one hundred degrees—no one gets that bored! Was it because these women were so remarkable? I love them both, but I would say rather it was because neither of them is very remarkable. And yet they have a remarkable story, because both have an incredible God.

"Vivian, how many women were at the meetings?" I asked.

"Dawn had the first group of about 350, I had the second group of about 250."

"I didn't know you were going to speak!" I gasped. "I thought you would do music and Dawn would speak!"

"So did I! But when we got there, Dawn felt that I was supposed to speak also."

"What did you say?"

"At first I didn't know what to say. I'd never been to prison. I thought I'd see a bunch of hardened criminals who could never care about me and my story."

"And?" I prompted.

"It was like talking with any other group of women. They didn't look different or act different. They were just in jail."

"So did you feel God used what you said?" I continued curiously.

"He used what we said, but I think He would have used any Christian testimony. Those women wanted to hear. They wanted to know if there was a way to find peace. Anyone with the answer could have told them."

"I'm so excited for you, Vivian!"

"It was so neat to be used! I felt like a part of what God was doing."

God was harvesting souls. Two former lesbians carried His message to help reap that harvest. All because they were available, sincere, and adaptable to the situation as God presented it.

Availability means that we are usable. But adaptability means we are capable and willing to make adjustments for God to use us in a given situation. Vivian needed adaptability when she was asked to speak, even though she wasn't anticipating it.

Dawn needed adaptability when she arrived at Jacksonville, planning on a quiet meeting with a base commander. "The day I flew in there was a front page news story about why I'd come—with my picture! That night it was on the 11 o'clock news. The next morning it was on the radio."

"Did you plan on all that publicity?" I asked.

"Not really. But I figured God knew what He was doing. I had personal reasons for being there, but God was using my story to tell others there are groups helping gays and lesbians change their lives. The news accounts also focused on my finding the answer to my lifelong search for affirmation and value in Jesus."

People heard about the change in Dawn's life through the media. That was a God-given opportunity to bring a gospel message of hope. But opportunity only becomes harvest when we make adjustments, allowing God to take our expectations and accomplish His will instead. Dawn thought she was there for one purpose; God had bigger plans.

Accountability

The rust-red track crunched beneath our feet in the early evening calm. Red-gold sunlight clung to the west, while twilight blue crept slowly up on the east. Dawn and I circled the track briskly and evenly. Somewhere along the way, I remembered Dawn had wanted to ask me about something. "What was it you wanted to talk to me about?" I asked.

"Well, " she hesitated.

Oh, no, Lord, I've done something wrong again, haven't I? I prayed.

Just listen.

"This isn't a big deal," she finally said. "But since I'm moving at the end of the year, I wanted to make sure everything was good between us."

"I've offended you," I had to struggle not to make it a sigh.

Most of my Christian life, I have worked to learn how *not* to offend people. If I were a quieter woman it would be easier. If I were not in leadership, I would be less visible and accessible. If I were not involved in a ministry where everyone seemed to be learning the ropes simultaneously, I would not always be slipping. Instead, I am an outspoken, high-profile pastor's wife whose feet seem as comfortable in her own mouth as they are in bedroom slippers. All excuses aside, I regularly offend people. This conversation has happened many times to me. Although over the years I have learned that the offense is not always my fault, I have also learned to admit when it is. Tonight God wanted me to learn something else.

"Well, sort of," she admitted. "You see, I've had to realize where I haven't allowed people to befriend me. Sometimes I push others away."

"I felt as if you did that with me a bit," I agreed. *Good,* I thought. *This sounds promising.*

"I did. But do you remember one day when we met at church and you made a comment about my makeup?"

"Oh, no, what did I say?" The creeping dread was upon me—*my fault this time.*

"You asked me who told me the eye shadow I was wearing looked good on me."

"I said that? How could I be so stupid? What did you say to me?"

"I didn't say anything. In fact, you came back and asked me if you'd offended me and I said, no."

"Dawn, I'm so sorry. Of course, I offended you," I apologized. "Will you forgive me?"

"Sure, it's okay."

Mona?

Yes, Lord.

You didn't offend Dawn, did you?

Sure I did. We both just agreed I did.

What did you really do?
What would that comment have done to you?

It would have hurt me. I hurt her!

That's right.
You can't use a word like *offend* if you want to break through the pain that's held you two apart.
You *hurt* her.

"Dawn," I began again. "I didn't offend you; I hurt you. No wonder you closed off our relationship. I'm really sorry. Will you forgive me?"

She nodded and smiled, "I forgive you."

"I never realized it before, but I use that question, 'Did I *offend* you?' when I feel convicted about *hurting* someone. It's a way to cover what I've really done and avoid their real feelings."

"Yeah, I guess I've never thought about it before," she agreed with my thinking.

We walked on in silence for awhile. As we did, I remembered a conversation I had had one day with John Smid, Love In Action's director. It was the same lesson God had just given.

"We like to use words that minimize the damage to our self-image, even when we know it is wrong," John said. "For instance, we say, 'I got a divorce.' What we really mean is, 'I abandoned my wife.' It's so much more comfortable for us to wrap the truth up in a cleaner package."

"But the problem with that is it isn't the truth," I said, following John's thinking.

"That's right. Someday there'll be a reckoning. If we've been kidding ourselves all along, we're in for a big surprise."

God was showing me something powerful about developing relationships with others. By letting the truth in, both Dawn and I were able to begin again, renewing our friendship. Dawn didn't merely want to find fault; she wanted to get at the bottom of the rejection she'd felt from me and find out if I was rejecting her or if I was just being thoughtless and unkind. Unilateral accountability was required to reap the healing in our friendship that we both wanted. She needed to say that she was hurt; I needed to see that I had hurt her. Then we could turn the corner and walk in the light.

What did I get for my humility? For being accountable? The psalmist answered my question: "Truth shall spring out of the earth; and righteousness shall look down from heaven" (Ps. 85:11).

Now, that sounds like a harvest worth reaping!

CHAPTER FIFTEEN

One Last Harvest: Decisions of Death and Life

Does Jesus care when my way is dark
With a nameless dread and fear?
As the daylight fades into deep night shades,
Does He care enough to be near?
Oh yes, He cares—I know He cares!
His heart is touched with my grief;
When the days are weary, the long nights dreary,
I know my Savior cares.[1]

As Bob sat down, the significance of the words he had just finished singing weighed upon my mind. Already very sick from AIDS, Bob spent days on end suffering with nausea and fever. There were nights he would lie awake praying for help. He had good cause to know that Jesus cared.

Words to a song mean nothing unless sung from the heart. These were. *Lord, this man is dying,* I thought. *He obviously believes every word. I've heard what his life has been like. Thank you for this incredible witness to your grace!*

How had this precious man come to such a dreadful pass in life? How had he come to a place of peace in his wretched circumstances? Was Bob Winter a "spiritual giant" or a brother like all the rest seated around me?

The Harvest Wears a Mask

Years ago, while on a vacation in Oregon, I went on a trail ride with my friend Connie. As we rode through farmlands and forested areas near her home in Portland, I could almost relive the easy days when we had ridden horses together as girls. At a new subdivision in various stages of construction, she pointed out an overgrown area. "I knew the farmer who lived here," she said. "He was getting old and finally sold the property. He realized he'd eventually be overpowered with the houses going up around him."

We rode closer to the old farm site. The buildings were all torn down; the land, newly graded. A few trees stood, but many had been removed. "What did he grow?" I asked.

"The best berries you've ever eaten," she replied, smacking her lips.

As we skirted the newly scraped land, we made our way toward the overgrowth at the rear of the farmer's old property line. The bushes came up to the stirrup leathers and grew densely along the path. I looked down and gasped, "These are the berry vines! They're covered with ripe berries!"

Truly, the old vines bent under the enormous load of fruit at its peak of ripeness. To this day, I am not certain what variety they were. Each berry measured two inches long and an inch across, was of deep purple color, and pungently tart and sweet together.

We rode home laughing and brought back a bucket brigade. No one minded as grownups and children alike scurried among the plants to pick the ripened fruit; the vines were soon to be removed. Stomachs and buckets loaded, we went home to can and bake. Rich dark jams and pie fillings emerged that night as Jack and Connie's kitchen became our production plant. Delectable smells pervaded every corner of the house, testifying to the harvest reaped. All from delicious berries hidden behind the mask of an unsightly, overgrown area in a new subdivision.

Bob Winter had similarities to the berry farmer's vines.

After accepting Jesus young in life, he grew up in the church and went to Bible college. He was a handsome, personable man with an easy, soft-spoken brand of charm. But within the seeming orderliness of his Christian walk, he harbored the growing belief that he had a problem too evil to talk about. Teenage homosexual experiences and confusion about his sexual identity collided with Christianity and spun Bob off into twelve years of involvement in the gay lifestyle.

By age thirty, dissatisfied and empty, he turned back to God for help. But struggles had only begun as Bob faced a boomerang from his former lifestyle: Just weeks after starting the road to recovery, his test for HIV antibodies was positive; now AIDS might well be in his future. What could he do? What would you do? Had he turned back to God only to learn that his life was over? Did Jesus care about the fear and grief he walked through?

Remember the berries? Hidden within the overgrowth of the old farmer's homesite lay one last crop. Ripened and ready to pick, they awaited one who could see and harvest them.

Bob Winter was a Christian man, a former homosexual, facing the specter of AIDS. But he was not ready to give up his life yet. Why not? For one thing, Bob knew that hidden within his life, which appeared to be scourged and spent, was a harvest waiting to be reaped. Throughout his short life, Bob had received much from the Lord. He had a lot to share with God's people. There was a crop to get in.

The Hope of Reaping

God has promised in Galatians: "For he that soweth to his flesh shall of the flesh reap corruption; but he that soweth to the Spirit shall of the Spirit reap life everlasting. And let us not be weary in well doing: for in due season we shall reap, if we faint not" (Gal. 6:8–9).

Bob Winter bravely faced a truth in his life. God was not to blame for his disease; he was facing the consequences of his own sins. His heart truly repentant, Bob acknowledged that the harvest of corruption he was reaping resulted from the body of death to which he had sown. The Author and Creator had warned of sin's destructive power. Bringing himself under God's authority, Bob surrendered totally to His justice.

Thankfully, God's justice is perfect. Bob knew that his sowing to the flesh yielded a harvest of corruption. Now there likewise would be a sure harvest of righteousness since he was sowing to the Spirit. God's justice would rejoice to prevail for good in a broken and humble life.

Bob went to churches and shared his story. He taught people the truth about the sin of homosexual activity. Testifying to God's Word, Bob warned many and simultaneously comforted others with hope for healing and change. In addition, he helped people see another side of AIDS and of the men and women suffering with it. He touched hearts hardened and embittered by fear with the simple humanity of his weakness. Disarming with his sincerity and vulnerability, Bob showed his Christian brothers and sisters an aspect of "ex-gay" ministry many had not known existed.

Finally, Bob shared with ministry leaders his vision for a Christian organization that would respond with the love of Jesus to anyone affected by any aspect of the AIDS epidemic. Now, years after his death, that vision has become reality as the Christian AIDS Services Alliance.

Bob Winter was a man with a sure future. God had designed him with a purpose in mind which would be fulfilled regardless of the outward appearances. As desperate as Bob's circumstances seemed, the Lord of the harvest had not given up on this vine of His planting. Bob's life served to build the lives of others. But what did he get out of it? Is there a reward for right? And, if so, what is that reward?

Redemption: The Reward of Right

"In the way of righteousness is life; and in the pathway thereof there is no death" (Prov. 12:28).

Over and over in the Bible, righteousness is linked with various rewards, but one reward underlies all. According to the Bible, righteousness leads toward life. Those who walk in its path walk toward life rather than death. The reward of right is redemption—never-ending life found only in Jesus Christ. We all long for this reward. Even as children we experience death in some form, and deep within we yearn for an escape from it. Aging, we confront more frequently the reality of approaching death. And yet, the hope of the gospel is this truth: Though we have been sold into death through sin, we are redeemed—bought back to never-ending life—by the death of Jesus Christ upon the cross.

Not only that, but the body of sin which enslaved us is put to death on that same cross. Now instead of sowing to that body of corruption, we begin to sow to the Spirit. Our very meaning and purpose is also redeemed.

Bob Winter had choices to make. Faced with death, he made the most profound choice for life. His life was redeemed. Though dying physically, he experienced God's forgiveness and love, and the Holy Spirit's indwelling power. Bob's physical struggle did not diminish. But the arsenal he fought with increased to the extent that he could face the troubles bravely.

But not all men and women faced with such choices decide to choose life. Even some who have known the Lord for many years turn away in their last days. Why? Sometimes their problem is as simple as driving in the wrong direction.

Turning It Around

What about you? As you read this, are you far away from God's blessing, looking wearily at the route back and wondering if you should take it? Are you infected with HIV or do you have AIDS? Do you think God has given up on you and you should give up, too?

Or perhaps do you know someone who is at this place in his or her life? Maybe you have just realized that you have harshly judged everyone who has taken the wrong road. God has made it so simple. We merely need to turn around and move in the right direction—toward life.

It is simple but never easy to get back onto the right road in the right direction. Our hurts and daily needs are too much to manage. It takes God to handle them. Sometimes we think we can deal with it all, but we are wrong. We are not God. So the longer we continue headlong down the road in the wrong direction, the more ground we will have to make up.

Letting Go of What Is Gone

Brianna came to the Love In Action women's live-in program from a life of incredible brokenness. Raped repeatedly in her adolescence, her image of herself as a woman was shattered. She did not want anything feminine; it had only caused her pain and humiliation. But she did want to be whole.

This is a hard thing for many "straight" people to understand: A lesbian woman may deeply long for the "normal" life of the heterosexual and still be repulsed by many aspects of that life. A gay man may want "normal" friendships with men and yet never feel comfortable in them.

Though Brianna wanted to desire what other women want, she was not able to make it happen. Why? Because Brianna's healing required her to forgive the man who had hurt her. She could not do it—or rather, would not.

Brianna wasted her energy wishing for something that could not be: She wanted her past to be different from what it was. However, God had a purpose for even the hardest things in her memories, if she had only trusted Him and allowed Him to work in her life.

The Problem with Playing Fair

"It isn't fair," she wailed. "I'm being punished for what he did to me and he isn't even having to deal with it."

"That's not true, Brianna. He will have to deal with it." I felt I was talking to a highway soundwall. This conversation happened repeatedly and the results were always the same. Brianna could not get past her unforgiveness, nor could she get on with her own life while clutching her bitterness.

She is like a woman struggling in the doorway of a burning house, trying to drag a sofa out with her. She screams again and again that the fire is hot and she's being burned—yet refuses to let go of her favorite piece of furniture.

Brianna would not let go. Rather than choosing an identity as a servant of Jesus and accepting whatever that meant in terms of sacrifice, she chose to go back into a lesbian lifestyle. "I know I'll wake up someday and hate myself," she told me shortly before exiting recovery and turning back in the wrong direction. "I know I can't be happy in the gay lifestyle. I'm just not willing to give up what I think is fair."

"And what is that, Brianna?" I asked, exasperated.

"He should be punished! I should be happy! Instead, it's the other way around."

We want God to be "fair" rather than just. What does that really mean? Fair means equitable, but that's not all it means. Fair carries with it the connotation of beauty from one's own perspective. In other words, fair is both equal and appealing. For most Christians, this means being blessed for the good we do. But Jesus warned that we would be persecuted for doing right. Also, fair would mean that those who do wrong *are not* rewarded for it. But in this world, often they are.

No matter how much we long for it, this life will never be fair! Nor has God promised that it will. What He has promised is justice. Like fairness, this word also means equity, but justice is impartial. In other words, the perspective of justice is God's, not any human's. God is not "a respector of persons"; He does not play favorites. His justice means that the balance will always be true.

If I follow God, He will account it for righteousness, no matter what the world thinks or says. Justice means that God sees my heart and knows my desire to serve Him, however I may fail and be misunderstood by those around me. It also means God alone will judge those who have wronged me.

What Might Have Been Never Was

Chris was a young man who, after leaving homosexuality behind, successfully completed the first year of Love in Action's live-in program. He became an integral part of our Sunday school. Everyone who met him enjoyed his upbeat approach and friendliness. Then Chris found out he was HIV-positive; eventually he would get AIDS. Everything changed.

His joy in serving God was completely overthrown by his despair in giving up all of his dreams and hopes for the future. How could he trust a God who would allow this to happen? In Chris' sight, we were all fools for not seeing the "truth" and for continuing to follow Jesus.

How could he turn around so completely and so quickly? He wanted something that could not be and refused to accept what was. He could not accept the sovereignty of God in allowing him to be infected with HIV, nor would he take responsibility for the sin that caused him to be infected.

Chris became angry and embittered against God and His servants. His earlier service was now eclipsed by his vehement denunciation of the church, the ministry of Love In Action, and the hope in Christ for healing from homosexuality.

To my knowledge, this brother has not returned yet to the Lord. He simply never came to see that his illness was the result of sinful choices he had made, contrary to God's commandments. But more importantly, he did not see that even if his illness were unrelated to homosexuality, God was still just. Chris needed a fresh view of God as the Author of his life.

Brianna and Chris are two examples of people who could not get past what they believed to be fair and get on with God's will in their lives. They did not trust His perfect justice.

Wanting the Lord to be something He is not, they looked for a God of circumstance. When the situation suggested that God was not "fair," Brianna and Chris refused to continue trusting Him. We tried repeatedly to argue for the truth, prayed for things to turn around, and then finally released them. But we have never forgotten or given up on them. Like the berry vines in Oregon and the testimony of Bob Winter, there is always hope for redemption. No matter how circumstances appear on the surface, the God of miracles still pursues us, desiring to turn defeat into victory!

Does Jesus care when my way is dark with a nameless dread and fear? By faith, Bob Winter believed He does. Like the great patriarch Abraham, Bob moved through his uncertainty toward where God called him: "By faith Abraham, when he was called to go out into a place which he should after receive for an inheritance, obeyed; and he went out, not knowing whither he went. . . . For he looked for a city which hath foundations, whose builder and maker is God" (Heb. 11:8, 10).

Every circumstance of life is like a road leading in two directions: toward God and away from Him. Bob Winter chose to turn around, follow the Lord, and allow his situation to glorify God and build His Kingdom.

Though the road ahead was obscured, Bob believed the One who led him on. Traveling through the deepening night, he kept his trust fixed upon the sure destination that other wanderers, like Abraham, have sought. In December of 1989, his work was done and his last harvest was brought in.

CHAPTER SIXTEEN

The Plowers and the Reapers: Unified Ministry for God's Kingdom

PENNY PEEKED INTO THE CHURCH. SEEING THAT IT APPEARED LIKE any other, she walked down the aisle to find a seat in a quiet spot. A stranger to this congregation, she felt out of place. *Oh well,* she thought. *It's a Christian church. This is my spiritual family, even if I don't know them.*

The music was beautiful. Many songs were the same as in her home church. *Imagine finding a church so comfortable!*

The pastor came to the podium. "Good morning," he beamed upon the congregation. His portly build and thick white hair reminded Penny of her own grandfather. Though she was sixty years old, she still remembered him fondly for his warm hugs and molasses candy. She smiled. *I'm so glad I came here this morning.*

The pastor's rich southern voice began to spin a story about his youth. "When I was a youngster we'd go camping in the woods back of our farm. The trees were all pines. We'd build a fire and pick up the cones and toss them in. In that part of the country, we called the pinecones 'faggots.' Some folks call a log for the fire a faggot, too. Now, you know, someday all these men who go around with other men are gonna be tossed into the fire and burned. And that's just what should happen."

Stunned and horrified, Penny slumped at the hatred this man was preaching. Though she agreed with the heart of his sermon on sin, she thought, *Lord, I think this man is saved. How can he get away with this kind of preaching?*

Did the pastor truly desire to see men and women turn from sin? Was he in touch with what God is doing? If he was a Christian, why did he harbor such an un-Christian attitude?

Without talking to him, there is no way to be sure what this church leader believes about men and women lost in homosexuality. We can be sure his approach will not help them turn away from wrong, though it may turn them away from God. And, if the Lord has called him to speak the gospel, how effective can he be if no one but saved people will listen?

This pastor needs a kingdom perspective! Rather than looking at gays and lesbians through the eyes of worldly fear, he needs to view them through the eyes of godly love.

You might wonder why I care. After all, the man does not understand the ministry we are involved in. So I should ignore him and go on, right?

Wrong! We *need* him! And not just for "ex-gay" ministry, either. Every believer needs a Christlike response in a day of deepening despair over lack of Christian values.

The heart of this response is the unity of true lovers of God. As days grow darker, we will discover our need to support each other more and more. But we should begin now. And what an appropriate issue to start with—helping the homosexual change. But it seems no one agrees on anything here. In fact the church is so polarized that all that's left is middle ground!

Unity—A Kingdom Perspective

"Behold, the days come, saith the LORD, that the plowman shall overtake the reaper, and the treader of grapes him that soweth seed; and the mountains shall drop sweet wine, and all the hills shall melt" (Amos 9:13).

God has promised an abundant harvest beyond our imagination. We are seeing it—but just the beginning. The secret of this kind of success in our work for God lies in the unity between churches and ministries that reach out to gays and lesbians. This unity can only be accomplished when leaders have a kingdom perspective on their tasks.

Think about the scene the verse from Amos describes—a time of so much plenty that as one crop is harvested, the field is being prepared for the next. The plower actually follows and overtakes the reaper because of the incredible increase. In other words, there is so much to reap that it cannot be done in time before the next season of plowing comes again.

For it to happen, excellent communication and cooperation must exist between the variously trained and gifted people at work. Imagine what would happen if the plowers were unaware that the reapers were even in the path. They might plow right over them! Or if someone had come already and planted seedlings? The plowers might destroy young plants simply because of ignorance.

All must work together in harmony—plowers, sowers, tenders, reapers, and treaders. When the plowers overtake the reapers and the sowers of seed overtake the treaders, then the work has become so harmonious and continuous that no effort will be wasted. But woe to workers who do not have unity! We all need each other, for none can reap except the field is plowed. And what about plowers with unplanted fields?

God cannot possibly bless us with this promised abundance until we are ready to work together to bring it in. How will that happen when we approach issues from such an opposite position as, for instance, the pastor described above?

First-century Christians provide us a good model. They had to deal with differences in the way they did things and the people they ministered to. How did they do it?

+ They examined to see what God was doing.

+ They applied to each new situation all they knew of the Lord's will.

Let's look at each of these ideas.

Examine God's Activity

The first Christians looked at their local situation to see what God was doing. That is what has been happening at Church of the Open Door. The results were unexpected, yet still led to a unity within the Body of Christ.

Mike Haley stood up and walked to the microphone. His usually ebullient personality was instead subdued and somber. Before he spoke a word, his face contorted with suppressed emotion.

Lord, this is so hard, I thought. *Why do we have to say good-bye?*

Tonight's evening service belonged to Love In Action. In four months, the ministry intended to move to a church a whole six states away. In recognition of the part Church of the Open Door had played for many years, they wanted an opportunity to express their feelings for our assembly.

"You may not think that you've affected our lives," Mike began. "But just watching you day to day as you came to church was healing to me. I saw how you scolded your kids when they needed correction and comforted them when they got hurt. Just the way you held their hands when they were too little to walk alone. All that helped me to be healed and grow, because those are things I felt I never had growing up. I'll always be grateful for things I've learned here."

His face clouded with emotion. "When I came here four years ago, I was a mess! I did everything I could to keep myself distracted so I wouldn't have to deal with things. But now I've been restored."

Mike had eventually addressed areas of his life where he needed healing. His growth continued when he joined Love In Action's staff. With the ministry move to Memphis, Tennessee, Mike planned to go as their admissions counselor, the first person many people would have contact with when they phoned or wrote for help.

I'm going to miss him so much, Lord.

I know.

What are you doing, God?

I'm giving the abundance I promised.
But it has caused this ministry to outgrow this church.
So I'm cutting it off and moving it to a new location
where it can continue to grow.

But what about us, Lord?

You are being pruned so new growth can emerge.

Over the twenty-plus years of our association, Love In Action had continued to expand until its people dominated the demographics of our church. Though emotionally difficult for both sides, the move would be healthy for both.

As Love In Action's leaders and the pastors of the church prayed, they realized this evening's meeting would come someday. By God's providential design, a church in Memphis, Tennessee, came forward and asked for the priviledge of hosting and fostering Love In Action.

In four months the Love In Action ministry would move across the country and relocate in Memphis. Besides the obvious advantages of a lower cost of living (with attendant lower real estate costs, food costs, etc.) and a large church body, there was the less evident expedient of a community more favorable to Christianity than Marin.

Christians here live in an extremely hostile spiritual environment. We do not doubt spiritual warfare goes on everywhere, but we know the daily toll it takes on us. Church of the Open Door has been under constant pressure and spiritual attack ever since we began some twenty years ago. As one area pastor put it with a sigh, "I know there are places where the darkness isn't so heavy. I just wish God would call me there."

The struggle is redoubled for a ministry like Love In Action. Its close proximity to San Francisco—a major stronghold of gay and lesbian support—causes increased tension in the lives of men and women trying to overcome their sin. If people are looking for a place to get involved in sin, they will find it in any city. But in the San Francisco area, it seems to come looking for you!

In addition, this region is extremely favorable politically toward homosexuality and unfavorable toward Christianity. We hope that Love In Action's move affords them the opportunity to reach more people and affect even greater change in the overall church community without being stifled in some of the ways they are here. And judging by the quality of their ministry staff, more impact is ensured.

Apply God's Will to New Situations

In dealing with their differences, the early church took all that they knew about the will of their Lord and applied it to each new situation.

As our evening "thank you" service continued, John and Anne Pauk stepped up to the microphone. After their wedding, they moved to another state. Though they were doing well enough in many ways, they were still very lonely for our fellowship. "Sometimes we lie in bed at night and wish we were back here with you," said John. "We miss you all so much." His lopsided smile was part joy and part sorrow as he continued. "I don't know why God has called us away, or what He has in store for us there. I know that we are where He wants us, though. But we really miss you guys."

Division is an important part of God's formula for the growth of His kingdom. Being a part of that kingdom means saying good-bye again and again. God has purposed to move our friends along in ministry. We could either release them cheerfully or grudgingly. But God loves a cheerful giver. He blessed our church for twenty years in helping gays and lesbians. Now He wants to bless someone else as well. Our job is to stay out of the way while He works. And His work is awesome!

Multiplication and Transplantation

Jesus Christ took twelve men. For three years He imparted to them His Father's plan to reach mankind. After His death and resurrection, much of what He taught began to bear fruit in the lives of these disciples. They, in their turn, continued His ministry, fanning throughout the world and sharing the message of His salvation.

God loves this kind of multiplication!

I witness to one person who becomes saved. That person witnesses to another who also becomes saved, and so on and on. In the context of a ministry like Love In Action, the testimony of one person can bring dramatic results in the lives of others. Many of them will change and, in their turn, testify to God's transforming power. But in order for new people to hear, some of us have to move to where those people are. We cannot all stay together and reach the world at the same time.

Highway 116 cuts across some of the most picturesque farm-land in California. Beginning in the heart of Sonoma's vinelands, it winds through the little towns of Cotati, Sebastapol, and Guerneville to finally intersect Highway 1 at the Pacific Ocean. Along the route, especially between Cotati and Sebastapol, lie many small businesses. Their weathered signs proclaim everything from antiques to fresh fruit, gravel to wood planters. The nurseries are my favorites. And of those, one that particularly caught my eye advertised "vintage" roses. I finally stopped one day and fulfilled the inner promise to learn more about these special plants.

Long lines of roses stood in the nursery beneath signs bearing their family names. Sunflowers, smiling out of huge tubs at the center of the enclosure, welcomed honey bees. A friendly breeze caressed leaf and petal, and lifted wisps of hair around my face. It was everything a nursery should be.

The nurserywoman spoke with authority, "Of course, no one really knows where the first rose came from."

"Do you start them all here?" I asked, somewhat uncomfortable that my lack of rudimentary knowledge of roses was hampering this interview.

"Yes, all of our roses are started from cane cuttings."

"My grandmother used to start roses that way. You just take a good branch from the rose and plant it, don't you?"

"That's right," she beamed.

Just like the roses in a huge ornamental garden, churches and ministries grow before the Lord, tended by His hand. Every once in a while He takes a cutting and transplants it in new soil. Though God loves multiplication, His kingdom often grows by division, too. That is what we are learning with the move of Love In Action. We look forward to see all that the Lord will accomplish through this plan.

The Plower and the Reaper

God desires to do so much! Just as the hint of a cloud and the whisper of a breeze on the prairie serve as only the merest suggestion of the cyclone on its way, the amazing things we have witnessed thus far only preface the downpour our Lord has promised.

There is a day coming when the harvest of gays and lesbians will be so abundant we will have to reap continuously just to keep up. But that kind of effort will require the cooperation of all men and women who serve God. Some will have big churches, like Central Church of Memphis. Others will call more modest places their church home, like the members of the Church of the Open Door in San Rafael.

We will be rewarded if we, like the earliest Christian churches and their people, look to see what God is doing, apply all that we know of His Word and His will to each new situation as it arises, and strive to be unified amongst ourselves in our desire to serve God in reaching the world.

Our God wants this harvest; we who reap fulfill His eternal plan. And one day the plower, sower, tender, reaper, and treader will all lay down their tools. God will welcome us to a thanksgiving feast. Sitting across the table from you or at your elbow may be some soul no one else cared about but you and God. Maybe you will have a chance to thank them for all they've taught you!

Resources

THANKFULLY, THERE ARE ENOUGH RESOURCE MATERIALS ON VARI-
ous aspects of both homosexuality and HIV/AIDS to fill a twenty-
page chapter! And more are being published all the time. So
although we could provide an exhaustive bibliography, all categorized by whether a particular book is best for men overcoming
homosexuality, women overcoming lesbianism, parents, wives,
etc., it seemed best that we simply refer you to organizations that
are experts in these fields. They keep a close watch out for new
materials available, and review them to see if they are worth your
buying or not.

Please contact the following referral organizations directly for
details on their practical bibliographies and resource lists. They can
also provide referrals to the closest ministries in your area that can
offer you support in whatever connections you face concerning
homosexuality and/or AIDS.

Referral Organizations

Homosexuality

Exodus International, P.O. Box 2121, San Rafael, CA 94912. Phone:
415/454-1017. Fax: 415/454-7826. Exodus also has a very large selection of
tapes from previous conferences available for purchase as well as articles,

bibliographies, and testimonies. Call or write them for an information pack. Their pack also contains helpful articles and testimonies.

HIV/AIDS-Related Issues

Christian AIDS Services Alliance (CASA), P.O. Box 3612, San Rafael, CA 94912. CASA offers a set of articles and bibliographies available for purchase. CASA referral members have permission to reprint most of these materials, and also receive a quarterly newsletter. They are planning a program for churches that welcome people affected by HIV.

Books and Resource Materials

Regeneration Books, P.O. Box 9830, Baltimore, MD 21284-9830. Order information line: 410/661-4337. Regeneration offers a mail order catalog of about sixty books on issues related to homosexuality, including books for men and women overcoming homosexuality; and for parents, spouses, and church leaders affected by these issues.

———

Christian General Store, 2130 Fourth St., San Rafael, CA 94901. Phone: 415/457-9489. The Christian General Store offers a catalog for mail, phone, and credit card orders of books on issues related to HIV/AIDS, and a selection of books related to homosexuality.

———

Americans for a Sound AIDS/HIV Policy (ASAP), P.O. Box 17433, Washington, DC 20041. Phone: 703/471-7350. ASAP is a public policy organization that also conducts a significant amount of AIDS education within the theologically conservative Christian community. They have excellent resource materials available on abstinence education, critiques of "safe sex," church HIV/infectious disease policy, medical issues, etc. They also offer topic searches in their extensive files.

———

The Barnabas Center for Emerging Issues, P.O. Box 3875, San Rafael, CA 94912. This is Brad Sargent's publishing ministry for resources on gender, sexuality, HIV/AIDS, worldviews, and men's studies. Extensive materials on AIDS ministry and on sexuality available.

———

True Love Waits, call 1-800-LUV-WAIT

———

Endnotes

Chapter 3
1. L. William Countrymen, *Dirt, Greed, and Sex* (Philadelphia: Fortress Press, 1988) opens up just such a possibility (see pp. 243–44).

Chapter 5
1. Adapted by permission from "What My Pastor Did Right" by Tim Rymel.

Chapter 11
1. Much of this chapter is condensed from my resource articles published by the Christian AIDS Services Alliance and The Barnabas Center.

2. Glenn G. Wood, M.D., and John E. Dietrich, M.D., *The AIDS Epidemic: Balancing Compassion and Justice* (Portland Oreg.: Multnomah Press, 1990), 272–73.

Chapter 12
1. Much of the material in this chapter comes from introductory articles in my extensive HIV/AIDS Resource Bibliography.

2. *The Essential AIDS Fact Book* (New York: Pocket Books, revised 1991), 8–9.

3. Judith Greif, M.S., R.N.C., F.N.P., and Beth Ann Golden, M.S.N., R.N.C., A.N.P. *AIDS Care at Home: A Guide for Caregivers, Loved Ones, and People with AIDS* (New York: John Wiley & Sons, 1994).

Chapter 15
1. "Does Jesus Care?" lyrics by Frank E. Graeff, 1860–1919, and music by J. Lincoln Hall, 1866–1930.